Endorsements

"If you're looking for a devotional that will draw you into the presence of Jesus, you'll want to pick up *Today Lord* by Dyann Shepard. With vulnerability and grace, Dyann walks you through the ups and downs of everyday life: the joys and sorrows, the gratitude and grumblings, he laughter and the tears, and the stops and the starts. This devotional will not only encourage your heart, but it will also deepen your walk with Jesus."

—Shelly Esser, Editor of *Just Between Us* magazine

"Dyann Shepard has a beautiful gift for helping readers see God's presence in the everyday moments of life. Through storytelling and heartfelt reflection, *Today Lord* reminds us that Jesus meets us not only in the extraordinary but in the ordinary places where love, loss, and grace intertwine. Each devotional feels like a personal invitation to slow down, look up, and encounter the Savior who walks beside us."

—Robyn Dykstra, National Speaker and author of *The Widow Wore Pink*

"*Today Lord* is a beautifully written collection of heartfelt reflections that will inspire and encourage you to seek Jesus in the everyday moments of life. Dyann Shepard's personal stories and biblical insights remind us of God's unwavering love and presence, even in the midst of life's challenges. This book is a gentle yet powerful invitation to deepen your faith and discover the hidden blessings God has prepared for you. It's a must-read for any woman longing to grow closer to her Savior."

—Carol Kent, Executive Director of Speak Up Ministries, speaker and author of *He Holds My Hand: Experiencing God's Presence and Protection* (Tyndale)

"Dyann Shepard writes with a tender heart and a keen eye for God's presence in everyday life. Her words invite readers to pause, notice, and encounter Jesus in the simple, ordinary moments that often go overlooked. With honesty and grace, she reminds us that every life matters deeply to God and that He continually calls us into a closer walk with Him. Her devotional reflections shine with hope, authenticity, and the quiet beauty of a faith lived out daily."

—Maggie Wallem Rowe, speaker and author of *This Life We Share*

"*Today Lord* is a beautiful collection of devotions that reveal the presence of God in ordinary moments. Using everyday experiences, Dyann brings out meaningful spiritual truth from simple life events and observations. Each devotion is easy to read, complete with Scripture, reflection questions, and a heartfelt prayer. It's a refreshing way to begin your day and encourages you to see God speaking through your ordinary moments."

—Peg Arnold, speaker, "Drama Queen for Jesus," author of *Devotions for the Distracted Heart* and *Making Your Message Memorable*

Today Lord

Encountering Jesus
in Ordinary Moments

Dyann Shepard

ISBN 979-8-9949135-0-5

Dedication

In memory of my husband Rick, the kindest of men.

I will always be grateful for his unconditional love and support.

Contents

Encountering Jesus in Our Sorrow

Encountering Jesus in Our Transformation

Encountering Jesus with Delight

Introduction

Small moments can teach us lifelong lessons if we will slow down and open our hearts to God. These teachable moments are revealed daily in the ordinary events we share as children of the Creator. I call these personal parables. They are easy to miss but priceless when we notice them.

I have a framed reminder in my home that says, "Make time for the quiet moments as God whispers and the world is loud." God reveals Himself in the ordinary, the shared life experiences we all encounter. Jesus taught using everyday examples of life through His parables.

Our shared journey is life: moments of joy and sorrow, loudness and quietness, victory and defeat, eventually physical death, but with the promise of eternal life to those who believe in Jesus Christ. As Solomon said in Ecclesiastes 3:1 (NIV), "There is a time for everything, and a season for every activity under the heavens."

God loves you and gave His only son, Jesus, for you. There is no greater love. He longs for you to receive Jesus as your personal savior and to have an intimate relationship with you. It is easy to keep our relationship with Jesus superficial, going to church, bible studies, etc., but there is so much more. Jesus prayed "that they all may be one, as You, Father, are in Me, and I in You; that they also may be one in Us, that the world may believe that You sent Me." (John 17:21 NKJV) This meaningful connection only happens when we invite Him into every circumstance and every event, including our anxiety, fear, and grief.

"Today Lord" is a collection of reflections and devotions from my life spent walking with, learning from, and listening to Jesus. When I opened my heart to Jesus on a daily basis, I discovered new gifts hidden in plain sight. My prayer is that you will be encouraged to listen for His voice and open your heart to His presence today and every day. He is waiting for you.

Hidden Gifts

Every branch in Me
that does not bear fruit
He takes away;
and every branch that bears fruit
He prunes, that it may bear more fruit.
(John 15:2 NKJV)

Hidden Gifts

Jesus loves you! These are the three most beautiful words we could ever hear. God's love for us, demonstrated through His Son, Jesus, is the most valuable present we will ever receive. It is not just for the beautiful, the young, or the perfect, but for everyone! It is forever. And there is nothing we can do to earn this great gift. But do we really believe that?

Sometimes I feel like I have to do or be something to earn God's love, but God says no. He loves me just the way I am. Scripture says, "We love, because He first loved us" (1 John 4:19). I love Him because He first loved me. He first loved you, too!

God expresses His love in many ways, most notably in the love of Jesus. Each day brings new opportunities to remember and experience His love.

For many years, the oak tree in my front yard was a daily visual of God's love for me. As I enjoyed my quiet time with the Lord each morning, I looked out at my tree. It was tall, sturdy, and shaded our porch and home. I loved my tree and what it provided.

Over the years, friends told me the main branch, which was the source of shade, was dead and needed to be removed. I couldn't let it go. A friend came by one day and announced he was cutting off the branch. I grieved! But afterward, to my surprise, the tree began to thrive. It looked different, but it had a new beauty, and it marked the beginning of many unique gifts of love, faith, trust, and provision.

Naturally, there was the provision of years of firewood. But there was a far more significant gift as well. With the branch gone, I saw something that had been hidden before: a beautiful heart etched deeply into the trunk where the branch had been. Over the next twenty years, I watched birds fly in and out of the heart as they sang their morning songs. That heart served as a sweet reminder from the Lord that when I cling too tightly to loved ones, possessions, the past, etc., I may miss a special gift from God.

In John 15:2 (ESV), Jesus said, "Every branch in me that does not bear fruit he takes away, and every branch that does bear fruit he prunes, that it may bear more fruit." How often I have clung to my old, dead branches. I usually resist when I feel the presence of the Lord's pruning shears. I want to hold on to my old branches. I am comfortable with them. They provide emotional shade for me.

However, this simple treasure, this heart etched into my tree, brought opportunities for me to share with clients and friends the gift of faith that grew from my tree. I've shared how the Lord stretched my faith when I began to "let go" of people and things precious to me so I could experience the joy of God's provision in my life and the lives of those I love. My children have matured spiritually and profoundly as I have ceased holding them too tightly.

One morning, my heart tree helped me let go of something I held dear, our church. I loved our church, the people, and the ministry I was involved with. When it became apparent my husband wanted to change congregations, I didn't want to let go. He didn't ask me to leave, but I knew he was unhappy. Privately, I cried and prayed.

As I sat in my prayer chair looking out the window at my heart tree, I asked myself if I was willing to put what I had learned to the test. Could I let go and trust that God had something new for me? After much struggle, I asked my husband to choose a new church. I told him, "As long as the people love Jesus, I'll be OK."

Many gifts were waiting for me at our new church. My husband was happier, more relaxed, and he grew spiritually, which was a great joy to both of us.

Still, I missed the teaching from my former church, which led me to reach out to friends and clients from various denominations to join me on a spiritual journey using only the Word of God. This adventure proved enormously rewarding. My walk with the Lord deepened in surprising ways.

I began attending a women's group at our new church. After a short message, we each find a quiet spot to meditate, pray, and journal. This meditative, thoughtful fellowship resulted in fresh growth and freedom in my faith walk with the Lord. It birthed a more profound peace and trust. I learned new ways of connecting with Jesus. I would have missed this sweet blessing with new sisters in the Lord if I hadn't been willing to let go of our previous church.

One morning, I looked at my heart tree and realized it was dead, the victim of drought. Once again, I cried, "No, not my special tree!" I didn't want to let go of the very symbol that had taught me to let go.

The morning the tree came down, my friend Ann brought me a book titled *The Giving Tree*. I read it through tears. Just as the tree in that book found a new purpose, so did my tree. The Lord sent us an excellent craftsman who preserved much of the trunk and all of the etched heart portion. He made a beautiful bench out of it for me.

My tree was repurposed! Now my heart bench serves as a reminder that as I walk in faith, God is faithful. He has a purpose with each season of my life.

What joy we experience when we see the heart of God in the daily blessings He bestows on us. Sometimes they are apparent, such as an answered prayer or a glorious sunset. Other times they are subtle, like in the smile of a stranger or a heart etched on a beloved oak tree.

Look for God's gifts for you. They are everywhere, waiting for you to recognize and receive them. You will be blessed as you discover these daily surprises of love.

Personal Reflection

- Am I holding on to something God wants me to let go of?

- When have I experienced a surprise gift from the Lord after letting go?

- How can I prepare myself today for something new?

Prayer

Today, Lord, give me eyes to see, ears to hear, and a heart open to new growth as You prune the old and make room for the new. May I delight in what You are doing in my life and be free of the fear that often comes with change. In the name of Jesus. Amen.

Scripture for Meditation

The LORD appeared to us in the past, saying: "I have loved you with an everlasting love; I have drawn you with unfailing kindness." (Jeremiah 31:3 NIV)

See, I am doing a new thing! Now it springs up; do you not perceive

it? I am making a way in the wilderness and streams in the wasteland.

(Isaiah 43:19 NIV)

To see a picture of the heart bench, visit:

www.personalparables.com/bench

Do You Love Me?

See what kind of love the Father has given to us,

that we should be called children of God;

and so we are.

(1 John 3:1 ESV)

Do You Love Me?

"Do you love me?" my three-year-old son asked the doctor. He was lying on a gurney, wide-eyed and filled with trepidation. He peered into the face of the stranger who was about to stitch up a deep cut over his eye, pleading for reassurance.

On the first day of preschool, my tiny but fearless child had gone down the playground slide on his tummy. His head caught a rough spot. The steel cut like a knife through his skin just above the eye.

The doctor paused when he heard Jonathan's innocent and heartfelt question, clearly startled for a moment. Then he smiled and responded, "Yes, in a generic sort of way."

I often ask the same question. Do you love me, God? I might not say it aloud or fully recognize the thought in my mind. But I ask it each time I'm fearful, experiencing disappointment, losing something, or in the midst of unexpected circumstances. The question lingers, and I wonder if God truly sees and knows what I'm going through.

God does not answer, "Yes, in a generic sort of way." He responds as a Father who loves me in a very personal way.

When I'm fearful and worried, my heart needs reassurance. Whenever I ask, "Do You love me, God?" He gently reminds me, "Yes, child, I love you." God's promises of His unique and great love for us are endless. His love is deeply personal. Like my three-year-old son, I sometimes look up for reassurance.

When you're feeling unsure of God's love, remember these promises from Scripture: Jesus leaves you with His peace (John 14:27), He will accomplish all that concerns you (Psalm 138:8), He knows the number of hairs on your head (Matthew 10:29-31), He knows your thoughts and the number of your days (Psalm 139:1-18), and He because of His great love for you, He gave His son (John 3:16).

Personal Reflection

- In what area of my life do I need reassurance?

- Will I let the truth of God's Word comfort and encourage me?

- Am I practicing being still before God long enough to hear His comforting voice?

Prayer

Today, Lord, I thank You for Your loving assurance. You surround me with Your love and protection. Help me to keep this truth in my heart and mind. Amen.

Scripture for Meditation

God shows his love for us in that while we were still sinners, Christ died for us. (Romans 5:8 ESV)

The steadfast love of the Lord is from everlasting to everlasting on those who fear him, and his righteousness to children's children. (Romans 5:8 ESV)

Letters from God

I know the plans I have for you, declares the Lord,
plans for welfare and not for evil, to give you a future
and a hope. Then you will call upon me and come
and pray to me, and I will hear you.
You will seek me and find me,
when you seek me with all your heart.
(Jeremiah 29:11–13 ESV)

Have you ever wished God would write you a letter that lays out your whole life and tells you exactly what to expect? Of course, we would want it to be full of good things: a happy marriage, perfect kids, financial security, and good health. But God, in His wisdom, chooses not to give us the details.

Knowing myself, if God had given me such a letter, I would not have read it to the end. I would have stopped at financial challenges, divorce, or children with their own willful minds. These were not part of my life plan. After reading halfway through, I would have said, "No thanks. Too hard. I didn't sign up for that."

Unlike us, Jesus did have the details. He knew all that He would suffer and the pain He would endure. He did it anyway. Hebrews 12:2 (NKJV) says He is "the author and finisher of our faith, who for the joy that was set before Him endured the cross, despising the shame, and has sat down at the right hand of the throne of God."

Jesus made this choice for you and me. Oh, the love of Jesus! We celebrate His resurrection and sing, "Hallelujah, what a Savior!"

That letter from God, which I so desperately wanted, seems like a bad idea now. If I had read only the first half, I would have missed the promise that God would be with me in the storm of my divorce. I would have missed the indescribable joy of my prodigal son returning and following Jesus wholeheartedly. I would have missed my loving thirty-one-year marriage to my husband, Rick.

Most importantly, I would have missed experiencing the profound faithfulness of God.

God is with you, whether your letter from Him includes a raging storm or a peaceful shore. He will not leave you or forsake you. This is the promise of God's Word, His complete letter to us. Hold tightly to His hand. He will lead and guide you to the end. Rejoice in His love!

- What area of my life do I need to give over to God's will?

- When I reflect on my past, where has God proven His faithfulness?

- Will I allow God to show me His faithfulness again by obeying His direction?

Prayer

Today, Lord, I confess I love control. I think I know how to run my life and how it should turn out. Forgive me. Your plans are always good and for my good. Remove my pride and allow Your promises and purpose to reign. Amen.

Scripture for Meditation

I know the plans I have for you, declares the Lord, plans for welfare and not for evil, to give you a future and a hope. Then you will call upon me and come and pray to me, and I will hear you. You will seek me and find me, when you seek me with all your heart. (Jeremiah 29:11–13 ESV)

Do not fear, for I am with you; do not be afraid, for I am your God. I will strengthen you, I will also help you, I will also uphold you with My righteous right hand. (Isaiah 41:10)

I am convinced that neither death, nor life, nor angels, nor principalities, nor things present, nor things to come, nor powers, nor height, nor depth, nor any other created thing, will be able to separate us from the love of God that is in Christ Jesus our Lord. (Romans 8:38–39)

You Are God's Poem

For we are His workmanship,
created in Christ Jesus for good works,
which God prepared beforehand
so that we would walk in them.
(Ephesians 2:10)

You Are God's Poem

Did you know you are God's masterpiece? Ephesians 2:10 says, "We are His workmanship created in Christ Jesus for good works, which God prepared beforehand, so that we would walk in them."

The Greek word translated as "workmanship" in that verse is *poiema*, which can mean a poem, a created piece of art, or a masterpiece. This reflects our uniqueness and our extraordinary place in God's heart.

I don't always feel like a masterpiece. When I spent three weeks in a recliner recovering from rotator cuff surgery, I did not feel valuable at all. I felt useless. I couldn't do anything worthwhile. I admit I had a few meltdowns during that time.

I'd made plans for those weeks, and they didn't include lounging in my comfortable chair. I anticipated working on some writing projects. I wanted to organize my closets and pictures. And I intended to help a friend as she was recovering from surgery. Now I was the one needing help.

But my surgery was not a surprise to God. He knew I needed to get my focus on Him instead of my plans. To be honest, I don't remember bringing my plans to the Lord. It didn't seem necessary.

A physical setback doesn't have to be a spiritual setback. God reminded me of the simple truth: wherever I am, He is. Unplanned events can provide precious moments with our Lord. During the time I was recuperating, God wanted me to take time to rest, relax, and enjoy His loving presence. I imagined Him tenderly rocking me in His arms as a mother soothing her child.

God reminded me that my worth is not in what I do. My value comes from being His child and what He says about me. Psalm 139:14 (NIV) says I am fearfully and wonderfully made by God. You are too! He created and designed us in His image.

How He uses us depends on His will and our willingness to be used in spite of our circumstances. Even in the midst of physical limitations, we can still worship. We can cultivate a grateful heart. We can pray for loved ones who are suffering from serious illnesses, loss, and financial difficulties. We can offer prayers and words of encouragement to our friends.

My prayers may be short when I'm ill, but they are heartfelt. I may tire quickly, but I can rest assured that God hears my prayers. And He receives my worship. He knows I'll be able to help in more tangible ways in the future.

God created me for good works, but I am not responsible for doing everything myself. In fact, by taking on too many responsibilities, I may be depriving other people of the blessing of fulfilling a need. This realization is humbling. But I am grateful for the friends and family the Lord has brought alongside me.

Those closets and pictures I planned to reorganize didn't need to be done right away. My writing projects could wait. What I needed most was for God to give me the wisdom to recognize what and who is most important.

Wherever you are right now, God is with you. He is for you. He loves you. You are His created piece of art, His poem, His masterpiece. You are precious in His sight. Rest in the sweet assurance of this truth.

Personal Reflection

- What areas of my life have I forgotten to turn over to God's control?

- What can I begin to do today to cultivate a grateful heart?

- What responsibilities in my life do I need to relinquish to someone else to make room for the priorities God has for me right now?

Prayer

Today, Lord, I give you thanks for creating me unique. Thank You that Your plan for my life to do good works is not to earn Your love but because of Your love. Remind me to give my plans over to You for confirmation and direction daily. Amen.

Scripture for Meditation

The Lord your God is in your midst, A victorious warrior. He will rejoice over you with joy, He will be quiet in His love, He will rejoice over you with shouts of joy. (Zephaniah 3:17)

Where can I go from Your Spirit? Or where can I flee from Your presence?

If I ascend to heaven, You are there; if I make my bed in Sheol, behold, You are there.

If I take up the wings of the dawn, if I dwell in the remotest part of the sea, even there Your hand will lead me, And Your right hand will lay hold of me.

If I say, "Surely the darkness will overwhelm me, and the light around me will be night," even the darkness is not dark to You, and the night is as bright as the day.

Darkness and light are alike to You. (Psalm 139:7–12)

Come now, you who say, "Today or tomorrow we will go to such and such a city, and spend a year there and engage in business and make a profit." Yet you do not know what your life will be like tomorrow. You are just a vapor that appears for a little while and then vanishes away. Instead, you ought to say, "If the Lord wills, we will live and also do this or that." (James 4:13–15)

Our God Is Present

For you shall go out in joy and be led forth in peace;

the mountains and the hills before you

shall break forth into singing,

and all the trees of the field shall clap their hands.

(Isaiah 55:12 ESV)

Our God Is Present

One morning, while walking near my home, I noticed pink and white blossoms on all the fruit trees. They weren't there the day before. As I drove around our little town, it was as if every tree had gotten the memo: "Burst forth!" The glorious sight reminded me of Isaiah 55:12 (ESV), "You shall go out in joy and be led forth in peace; the mountains and the hills before you shall break forth into singing, and all the trees of the field shall clap their hands."

I saw and felt God's presence everywhere. Of course, God was present the day before as well. But I didn't have the eyes to see. I couldn't feel His presence in the same way. One of the Hebrew names for God is Jehovah Shammah, meaning The Lord Is Here. The Lord is present, even when I can't feel Him or see His work.

When I took the same walk the day before, tiny buds were on the branches. The branches were attached to the tree trunk. Below the ground's surface, unseen roots nourished the trunk that fed the branches that produced the little buds. It was all there, even though I hadn't noticed. But the fact that I didn't see it did not change the truth of the presence of life, nourishment, and God's glory, which was about to explode into sight.

Had the tiny buds been cut off from the branches, they would never have been able to serve their purpose, which was to blossom and bear fruit. This is true for me when I do not stay connected to Jesus, my source of life. In John 15:5 (NKJV), Jesus told His disciples, "I am the vine, you are the branches. He who abides in Me and I in him, he bears much fruit, for without Me you can do nothing." I may not see or feel God working, but He is. Even when I feel spiritually dormant, He is preparing, nourishing, and cultivating the soil of my soul as long as I stay connected to Him. He takes me through the various seasons of life just as He does the fruit trees.

There is purpose in the trees' dormant period. Fruit trees that do not go into winter hiatus will not grow well and produce a good yield. Our dormant times are for resting, reflecting, and being refreshed in the roots of our souls. These seasons may be difficult, but our spiritual fruit will not mature into Christ's sweet taste and aroma without them. We will not appreciate the sweetness of God's presence.

When Jesus was crucified, the disciples thought all was lost because their Lord was gone. But He wasn't. He was waiting to burst forth from the tomb. The disciples couldn't see Him and didn't feel His presence, but that did not change the fact that Jesus was about to demonstrate life and victory over death. What an awesome God we serve!

Is it possible to fully grasp our amazing God? Scripture declares that He is our salvation, our refuge, our strength, our joy, our substitute, and our shepherd. He is the way, the truth, and the life. (John 14:6) He is Emmanuel, God with us. (Matthew 1:23)

As you celebrate Jesus's victory over death, which led to your eternal life, choose a name or adjective that describes God to you. Ask the Lord to reveal the truth of that name in your daily life.

The tomb is empty! Come, let us worship Him.

Personal Reflection

- What am I actively doing to prepare the soil of my soul during dormant spiritual times?

- What am I doing to nourish my soul during times that feel dry?

- How am I cultivating my soul and preparing for new growth?

Prayer

Today, Lord, I give you thanks for the truth of Your presence, even when I don't feel or see You. Help me to stay in the Word and in prayer and to have a grateful heart regardless of how I feel. Remind me to stay connected to You, my source of life. Amen.

Scripture for Meditation

Read **Psalm 139** and **Psalm 8** as you contemplate the goodness and presence of the Lord.

Jesus said to her, "I am the resurrection and the life. He who believes in Me, though he may die, he shall live. And whoever lives and believes in Me shall never die. Do you believe this? (John 11:25–26 NKJV)

Hang On and Let Go

Let's hold firmly
to the confession of our hope
without wavering,
for He who promised is faithful.
(Hebrews 10:23)

Hang On and Let Go

I sometimes visualize myself as a child on the monkey bars. As I swing from one bar to the next, I have to keep the momentum going. Between bars, there's a brief moment when I am suspended in the air. I have to let go of the previous bar before I can grasp onto the next one. If I look down, I'll fall. But if I keep my eyes on the next bar and stretch, I will catch it just after I let go of the one behind. I cannot hold on to the old and grab the new at the same time.

When I was twenty-two years old, a teacher told me, "There are times when you must hold on to Jesus for dear life." At the time, I thought he was being a bit dramatic. But when my life spun out of control and fell apart, I had to reach for Jesus and hold on to Him while letting go of the life I knew.

I am a woman of habit, structure, and consistency. I like control. I am independent, reliable, and responsible. I am also stubborn and unwilling to try new things. I lose out on many lessons and blessings because I hold too tightly to my familiar routine and plans.

When the Lord lets me know I need to let go of something in my life, my first reaction is to scream, "No! My plans are good, even godly." But as time passes, I realize that my "good" plans are not God's best plans for me.

For a while now, I have attended about four conferences for writers and speakers each year. But my family circumstances have changed, and I'm needed at home now. So, this year, I will attend only one.

As I strive to accept letting go of my plans, I recall other times when I let God provide as I clung to Him.

- When a unique and beautiful shade tree in my yard died, God had a hidden heart-gift waiting for me.
- When I left my beloved church home, God provided a new church family for me, which became the catalyst for my falling in love with writing and speaking.
- After I let go of my first marriage, the Lord provided my wonderful husband, Rick.

- I had to hang on to Jesus when my son was placed into the juvenile system, but later I was blessed by his renewed faith in the Lord.

Remembering God's faithfulness strengthens me as I trust Him for the future. The children of Israel had to let go of family and land more than once. Each time, God provided their needs. Often, He directed them to build an altar to commemorate the event. Its purpose was to help them remember God's faithfulness and worship Him each time they passed by. It was to remind them that He is trustworthy, even with an unknown future.

When I hold on to Jesus, regardless of the circumstances, He reveals a path filled with surprises and gifts prepared for me. Most of the time, I go kicking and screaming. But when I let go, I find an unexpected blessing.

When my ideas are halted, changed, or diverted, I look back at God's faithfulness and provisions. That makes it easier for me to exchange my plans for His. I experience a refreshing peace of acceptance.

Personal Reflection

- Is there something God is asking me to let go of as I hang on to Him?

- Why am I afraid to let go?

- What "altar of remembrance" do I need to erect to help me trust Jesus with my future?

Prayer

Today, Lord, I give You thanks for Your faithfulness. You have ordained my days. Your plans are perfect. Open my eyes to the path You have chosen for me. Reveal to me when I must let go of my will to reach for the joy You have waiting for me. Thank You for Your patience. Amen.

Scripture for Meditation

"For My thoughts are not your thoughts, nor are your ways My ways," says the Lord. "For as the heavens are higher than the earth, so are My ways higher than your ways, and My thoughts than your thoughts." (Isaiah 55:8–9 NKJV)

Let's hold firmly to the confession of our hope without wavering, for He who promised is faithful. (Hebrews 10:23)

Cling tightly to the Lord your God as you have done until now. (Joshua 23:8 NLT)

Is Your Life Ebbing or Flowing?

Do not boast about tomorrow,
for you do not know what a day may bring.
(Proverbs 27:1)

Is Your Life Ebbing or Flowing?

Three years ago, my life was flowing in all the ministries I felt God was calling me to: writing, speaking, family, and church life. I was excited as I worked on my second book and study guide on aging. But my plans changed quickly when my dear husband became very ill. He became my ministry, one I was privileged to have and happy to accept. During this challenging season, I learned a lot about myself, my husband, and the faithfulness of God in the midst of trying times. There is something profoundly beautiful about handing over your loved one's earthly life in exchange for their eternal one.

The flow didn't return quickly after my loss. There was much to deal with: the shared grief of family and friends, the celebration of life, paperwork, personal items, grief classes, and an empty, quiet home. I soon realized my house was too large for me. So I invited my son and daughter-in-law to move in with me, which was a tremendous blessing. And I converted my office into a little studio for me.

When I felt ready to flow again, I returned to my plan and began to work on my book, as well as accepting several speaking engagements. However, to my surprise and disappointment, there were more delays. First, there was cataract surgery on both eyes, which set me back a month. Next, as I was leaving on a mini vacation with my girlfriends, I had a fluke accident, fell, and broke off the top of my femur; another month lost. I thought, *Good grief, Lord, did I misunderstand Your calling on my life? Is there something I need to learn that I missed earlier?*

Do you ever ask that question when your plans are diverted? It's difficult to understand delays, especially when your plans are to minister and serve the Lord. Our human nature protests, and we ask, "Why?"

I had a lot of time to think, pray, and question my calling while in the hospital. I thought surely the Lord would reveal a new lesson for me. I waited for that "ah-ha" moment when the spiritual light would go on, the big life-changing revelation.

But none came.

As I reflect on the past three years, I realize God is always quietly reminding me of His promises. I don't need a huge revelation. I need to replace the "why?" with "how?" *How then shall I live, Lord?* I need to meditate on what God reveals in His Word to be true yesterday, today, and tomorrow (Hebrews 3:8).

Scripture assures me that I am living in the will of God when I practice the following:

- In everything give thanks, for this is the will of God for you in Christ Jesus. (1 Thessalonians 5:18)

- Not that I speak from want, for I have learned to be content in whatever circumstances I am. I know how to get along with humble means, and I also know how to live in prosperity; in any and every circumstance I have learned the secret of being filled and going hungry, both of having abundance and suffering need. (Philippians 4:11–12 NASB 95)

- Cease striving and know that I am God. (Psalm 46:10 NASB 95)

The question "How then shall I live?" is answered in the two great commandments from Matthew 22:36–40, which are to love the Lord your God with all your heart, with all your soul, and with all your mind, and to love your neighbor as yourself.

Life is made up of ebbs and flows, grumbling and gratitude, joy and sorrow, laughter and tears, starts and stops. We must choose whether we will sit in our sorrow or surrender to God's will, timing, and grace, whether we understand or not.

My prayer is to experience daily Psalm 131:2 (AMP): "Surely I have calmed and quieted my soul; like a weaned child [resting] with his mother, my soul is like a weaned child within me [composed and freed from discontent]."

Personal Reflection

- What areas am I clinging to that God is asking me to surrender to His will?

- What one promise of God can I begin practicing today?

- How am I intentionally resting in the arms of my heavenly Father?

Prayer

Today, Lord, thank You for reminding me that Your plans are always good, even when my plans are put on pause or permanently diverted. Help me to trust You in the ebbs and flows of life, knowing that You see my life in full while I see only what's behind me and right in front of me. Teach me to accept Your will and to give You thanks in all circumstances. Amen.

Scripture for Meditation

Do not boast about tomorrow, for you do not know what a day may bring. (Proverbs 27:1)

"For I know the plans that I have for you," declares the Lord, "plans

for prosperity and not for disaster, to give you a future and a hope."

(Jeremiah 29:11)

Little Places

Brothers and sisters, think of what you were
when you were called.
Not many of you were wise by human standards;
not many were influential; not many were of noble birth.
But God chose the foolish things of the world to shame
the wise; God chose the weak things of the world to
shame the strong. God chose the lowly things of this
world and the despised things and the things that are not—
to nullify the things that are,
so that no one may boast before him.
(1 Corinthians 1:26–29 NIV)

Little Places

I was very blessed to have praying grandmothers. They lived humble and unpretentious lives. By much of the world's standards, based on power, wealth, and fame, they lived insignificant lives. But to me, and more importantly to God, their lives were hugely significant because they lived for Him.

Grandma Goforth, my maternal grandmother, never drove a car and was orphaned at six, but she loved Jesus. She lived a simple life and prayed faithfully. She was kind, gentle, and loving. When her husband died, she got a job and worked for twenty years. It took two people to replace her when she retired.

Every summer, I took the Greyhound bus to Glendale and spent a week with her. I loved these special times. She always had ice cream bonbons and ginger snaps waiting for me when I arrived. We played pick-up sticks and read together. We walked to Baskin-Robbins and took the red bus to Bob's Big Boy for hamburgers and chocolate malts. She wasn't famous. She wasn't what the world would call a success. But she had a profound influence on my life. I remember every room in her home, the pictures on the walls, the furniture, and the blue willow dishes we always used.

She died before I could tell her how grateful I was for her love and prayers. But the ripple effect of her life lives on in me, my children, and my grandchildren. I hope her influence also pours over to my friends and acquaintances. Though I'm sure she never knew it, she was the woman I've strived to be.

After my grandma died, I found little notes wrapped around some of the few earthly possessions she had. These writings were sometimes addressed to me, telling me the item's history. Inside her journal, a ragged, beat-up binder, were treasures of her prayers and thoughts. She wrote prayers for my parents, me, and my brothers. Each page reflects her heart and love for God. She enlarged my life with her presence and continues to expand it through her memory and the few mementos I have of hers. She was a sweet aroma of Christ.

I discovered a poem in her journal called "Little Places." I have copied it below for your reflection. This poem always reminds me that what I consider little becomes great in God's hands. When we make what we have available to God, He takes it, blesses it, and multiplies it beyond our wildest imaginations. We see this principle in Scripture when Jesus fed the five thousand with the five loaves of bread and two fish given by a young boy. The boy was not concerned about his offering being too little to be helpful. In the hand of God, it was more than enough.

When we present to the Lord what we do have, tiny as it may seem, He will take our offering and do something incredible with it. We may never know the end result. My grandmother didn't realize how her gift of time and love helped transform my life. We don't need to know the outcome. God wants us to give our offerings and leave the results to Him.

LITTLE PLACES

By Meade McGuire

"Master, where shall I work today?" My love flowed warm and free.

He pointed out a tiny plot and said, "Tend that for Me."

I answered quickly, "Oh, no, not there. Not anyone could see.

No matter how well my task was done, not that little place for me."

His voice, when He spoke, it was not stern. He answered me tenderly.

"Little one, search that heart of thine. Are you working for them or Me?

Nazareth was just a little place, and so was Galilee."

- What areas of my life is God asking me to offer in faith?

- What opportunities to bless someone have I missed because I thought my gifts were too small or insignificant?

- What is one simple action I will do today to bless and encourage someone?

Prayer

Today, Lord, remind me that You multiply my gifts to bless and provide for others. You often choose what appears to be a meager offering to become a significant provision in someone's life. Give me eyes to see the needs of those around me. Give me the vision to offer what I have, no matter how small, and leave the result to You. Amen.

Scripture for Meditation

Whatever you do, work at it with all your heart, as working for the Lord, not for human masters, since you know that you will receive an inheritance from the Lord as a reward. It is the Lord Christ you are serving. (Colossians 3:23–24 NIV)

He looked up and saw the rich putting their gifts into the treasury, and He saw also a certain poor widow putting in two mites. So He said, "Truly I say to you that this poor widow has put in more than all; for all these out of their abundance have put in offerings for God, but she out of her poverty put in all the livelihood that she had." (Luke 21:1–4 NKJV)

God's Golden Threads

Whatever you do, work at it with all your heart,
as working for the Lord, not for human masters,
since you know that you will receive
an inheritance from the Lord as a reward.
It is the Lord Christ you are serving.
(Colossians 3:23–24 NIV)

I love reading biographies. Learning about the journey of someone I admire is fascinating. Their path is rarely a straight line. It's marked with twists and turns, success and failure, encouragement and discouragement. The patterns and pieces come together only in life's rearview mirror.

I often forget God is creating a tapestry of my life. When I encounter a blind curve or unexpected disappointment, I need to remind myself that I am God's beloved and that Romans 8:28 (NKJV) applies to me: "And we know that all things work together for good to those who love God, to those who are the called according to His purpose."

This verse is not a promise that everything we experience will be good, but that God will produce something good when we love Him and yield to His purpose.

When discouragement sets in, I begin to feel like I am not enough. I question whether my life really matters to my heavenly

Father. Allowing these thoughts to take root can lead me into the dangerous trap of comparing myself to others and measuring my sense of self-worth by the worldly view of value through accomplishments, financial success, or influence. God never uses these labels to define me. I am His child, His beloved. Always.

The Lord continually reminds us through Scripture that our lives, words, and thinking matter. All three are interrelated and are part of the ripple effect of our existence. Like a pebble thrown into the pond, we often see only the immediate results but not the final destination. We are valuable to God. We influence our friends, family, colleagues, and future generations. From our limited vantage point, we only see where we have been and where we are. We do not see the complete journey before us. We may have assurance of our ultimate heavenly home, but the path to our eternal dwelling may be full of blind turns and scary shadows. We live in the unknowns of faith as described in Hebrews 11:1 (ESV), "Faith is the assurance of things hoped for, the conviction of things not seen."

I like to think of our lives as golden threads that bind people and events together in ways that shine and reflect God's love and glory.

I saw this parallel clearly when I learned about the lives of Tobias and Ollie Ham. Their names don't appear in any list of the top 100 most influential people. Nor is their son Mordecai well known in modern Christian circles. But God wove a golden thread through them for His future kingdom.

Tobias Ham was a farmer in southern Kentucky. He and his wife, ("Ollie"), had six children. Each night, Tobias faithfully read Scripture to his family. Their son Mordecai became an evangelist, and through his ministry Billy Graham became a Christian. Tobias and Ollie could not have imagined their faithful family Scripture reading would result in more than 215 million people hearing the gospel of Christ through the Billy Graham crusades.

As I read about the lives of Tobias, Ollie, and Mordecai, I thought about some of the people who have woven golden threads into my life. My faith is the direct result of my grandmother's influence. She was poor and was not educated past eighth grade. But her Christlike example of love, simplicity, and humility carved a path of faith in me.

My first boyfriend's mother, Fran, was a gracious example to me of the forgiveness and mercy of Christ. Instead of complaining about her loss from a home invasion robbery, she prayed for the intruders. She was concerned that they didn't understand the love and forgiveness of God.

These dear women loved their heavenly Father and sought to live sincere, godly lives. I am the beneficiary of their faithfulness.

You may not influence the next Billy Graham. Or who knows? Maybe you will! But as you live for the Lord, your life can be part of the continuum of a golden thread in the lives of others. A simple smile to a stranger can change their day; it may even be an answer to their prayer for someone to notice them. As we drive by the scene of a car accident, we can whisper a prayer for anyone who may be injured. When we notice a person who looks lost and lonely, we can pray for them to turn to the Lord. Prayers like these will reach the heart and ear of God.

As we practice the presence of God, our life transforms into the image of Christ. When we live as the beloved of the Lord, we have the privilege of participating in His transforming work in the lives of others.

First Corinthians 13:12 (ESV) states, "Now we see in a mirror dimly, but then face to face. Now I know in part, then I shall know fully, even as I have been fully known." God is doing mighty things in and through us as we choose to be faithful and trust Him no matter what. When we allow God to weave His golden threads into our lives, we are privileged to be part of the unseen but magnificent future tapestry of others.

"Your faith may be just a little thread. It may be small and weak, but act on that faith. It does not matter how big your faith is, but rather, where your faith is."[1]

---

[1] Franklin Graham with Donna Lee Toney, eds., *Billy Graham in Quotes* (Nashville: Thomas Nelson, 2011), 136

- In what area of my life can I begin to practice the presence of God in a new way?

- What golden threads can I identify in my life?

- What can I learn by reading about the lives of Christians who have gone before me? Suggested reading: research the life and ministry of Henrietta Mears, a chemistry teacher from Fargo, North Dakota.

Prayer

Today, Lord, I thank You for all the saints who went before me. The ripple effect of their lives impacted mine. Remind me that my life can influence others for Christ at home, work, or school. Keep my focus on allowing You to transform and renew me as I trust and follow You. Thank You for taking the golden thread of my life and using it in the lives of others, even those unknown to me.

Scripture for Meditation

Now to Him who is able to do far more abundantly beyond all that we ask or think, according to the power that works within us, to Him be the glory in the church and in Christ Jesus to all generations forever and ever. Amen. (Ephesians 3:20–21)

Whatever you do, work at it with all your heart, as working for the Lord, not for human masters, since you know that you will receive an inheritance from the Lord as a reward. It is the Lord Christ you are serving. (Colossians 3:23–24 NIV)

Grace and Joy
in an Unexpected Easter

He looked up and saw the rich putting their gifts

into the treasury, and He saw also

a certain poor widow putting in two mites.

So He said, "Truly I say to you that

this poor widow has put in more than all;

for all these out of their abundance have put in

offerings for God, but she out of her poverty

put in all the livelihood that she had."

(Luke 21:1–4 NKJV)

Grace and Joy in an Unexpected Easter

Many years ago, while my husband and I were out of town over Easter weekend, we decided on Sunday morning to look for a place to worship. At each church we came across, we just missed the start of service. Finally, we found a small church in the old section of Salinas, California.

The congregation was an eclectic assortment of people. Some were dressed in their Easter finest, but many looked like homeless people just off the street. The man next to me was disheveled and missing most of his teeth.

But I sensed a simplicity and tenderness to this church. As we sang a familiar hymn, I looked over at the man beside me. Tears were running down his cheeks.

At that moment, I understood: he was my brother. We were part of the same family. We were both God's children—not because of who we were, what we had, or what we did, but solely based on who Christ is and what He has done for us.

When the song ended, a woman ran down the aisle praising God loudly. She was tall, dark, wearing a purple robe, with a big turban around her head, and a blond ponytail off to the side. Another woman, dressed in a beautiful yellow suit, jumped out of her seat, ran after her, and threw her arms around her. As the woman in yellow held her in a warm and loving way, I sensed this was a holy moment.

When the offering plate was passed, the pastor announced this week's provision was for four churches in the community that were struggling. It brought to mind the passage from Scripture of the poor widow whose small offering was more valuable in Jesus's eyes than all the others. "They all contributed out of their abundance; but she, from her poverty put in all that she had to live on" (Luke 21:3–4 ESV).

We left the Salinas service with a profound sense of God's Spirit. We were reminded that, as beautiful as Easter pageants, lilies, and choirs are, our God is in the simple. Our worship is not dependent on presentation; it is only dependent on the presence of Christ.

That year, we experienced a different kind of Easter, worshipping alone without family or friends. It was a lonely time. But then, the cross was lonely.

The future may present other Easters that are spent alone due to illness, age, or some unforeseeable circumstance. I am grateful for the experience of the Easter service in Salinas. It taught me that even in the unexpected and the unplanned, God will always meet me.

He will always meet you, too. As you open yourself to the holy presence of Christ, you will experience grace and joy. God is with you regardless of the place of worship, because the fact is that God loves you. Jesus died for you and rose for you. He is victorious. Wherever you are today, rejoice!

Personal Reflection

- How can I be more open to God's blessings when I encounter an unexpected change of plans?

- When was the last time I found the joy of worship in a simple act of love and acceptance?

- Will I intentionally choose to see Jesus in the face of "the least of them: the poor, the rejected, the disenfranchised"?

Prayer

Today, Lord, I confess I often miss Your blessings because of my predetermined expectations. Please give me Your eyes to see, Your ears to hear, and an open heart ready to receive whatever and whomever You set before me. I am grateful for Your patience as I seek to be more like You. Amen.

Scripture for Meditation

Give thanks in all circumstances; for this is the will of God in Christ Jesus for you. (1 Thessalonians 5:18 ESV)

He looked up and saw the rich putting their gifts into the treasury, and

He saw also a certain poor widow putting in two mites. So He said,

"Truly I say to you that this poor widow has put in more than all; for

all these out of their abundance have put in offerings for God, but she

out of her poverty put in all the livelihood that she had." (Luke 21:1–

4 NKJV)

What Fragrance Are You Wearing?

Be imitators of God, as beloved children.

And walk in love, as Christ loved us

and gave himself up for us,

a fragrant offering and sacrifice to God.

(Ephesians 5:1–2 ESV)

What Fragrance Are You Wearing?

Taking walks around our lake is one of my favorite pastimes. Often, a woman or young girl will pass by, leaving a lingering fragrance—a sweet aroma of citrus or florals that hangs in the air. I hope to pass her again on the other side to ask her what perfume she is wearing.

I wonder what kind of fragrance I leave when people encounter me?

Scripture describes us as a fragrance of Christ (2 Corinthians 2:15). God wants a sweet scent to flow from us and permeate the space around us. What a thought. When we walk by someone, do they think, *Wow, she smells so sweet,* even when we are not wearing perfume? Does the aroma of Christ linger in a room after we exit? Does anyone ask where that delicious scent comes from?

The Bible often describes our relationship with our heavenly Father through our five senses. In addition to our sense of smell, scripture tells us to *taste* and *see* that the Lord is good (Psalm 34:8).

When we *hear* Him, we are to follow. Jesus told Thomas to *touch* His hands and feet (Luke 24:39). The Lord asks us to use our senses to experience Him, know Him, and spread His love.

The Spirit's fruit is love, joy, peace, patience, kindness, goodness, faithfulness, gentleness, and self-control (Galatians 5:22-23). God's list of fruit starts with love, because God is love (1 John 4:8). From His love springs the remainder of the fruit, culminating in self-control. When we cultivate and nurture the fruit of the Spirit, we help reproduce those qualities in ourselves and others.

In the physical realm, fruit has seeds for reproduction. Spiritual fruit has the same purpose. We are Christ's fragrance in a world filled with despair. Maybe today we will be like a crisp apple that refreshes someone's soul. Or the soothing comfort of warm lemon tea as we listen to the heavy burden they carry.

I often ask myself, What fruit am I cultivating? Are they sweet to the soul? Do they exude a fragrance of love, joy, and kindness? What am I filling my soul with to reproduce good, refreshing, delightful fruit in myself and others? What needs to be picked off, pruned, and composted? I pray that my ears will be open to the

answers from my Lord.

Personal Reflection

- Which fruit of the Spirit do I need to cultivate today?

- How has the fragrance of Christ in others impacted my own life?

- How can I cultivate the aroma of Christ to share with others?

Prayer

Today, Lord, reveal to me new ways to cultivate the fruit of Your Spirit. Help me to leave the fragrance of Christ with each person I encounter. Amen.

Scripture for Meditation

The fruit of the Spirit is love, joy, peace, patience, kindness, goodness, faithfulness, gentleness, self-control; against such things, there is no law. (Galatians 5:22-23 ESV)

But thank God! He has made us his captives and continues to lead us along in Christ's triumphal procession. Now he uses us to spread the knowledge of Christ everywhere, like a sweet perfume. Our lives are a Christ-like fragrance rising up to God. But this fragrance is perceived differently by those who are being saved and by those who are perishing. To those who are perishing, we are a dreadful smell of death and doom. But to those who are being saved, we are a life-giving perfume. (2 Corinthians 2:14–16 NLT)

What's On Your Head?

Set your mind on the things above,

not on the things that are on earth.

(Colossians 3:2 NKJV)

What's On Your Head?

"Come on," the quarterback yelled. "Get your mind right. Let's go!

The team was behind, and they couldn't afford to lose focus. Their leader told them to forget the last play and concentrate on getting this next play right.

The apostle Paul says the same to us in 2 Corinthians 10:5 (NKJV) when he speaks of "casting down arguments and every high thing that exalts itself against the knowledge of God, bringing every thought into captivity to the obedience of Christ." And in Philippians 3:13–14 when he says, "One thing I do: forgetting what lies behind and reaching forward to what lies ahead, I press on toward the goal for the prize of the upward call of God in Christ Jesus."

In these Scriptures, God urges us to forget past failures and disappointments. We need to get our minds right and focus on what's ahead. Thoughts of doubt, temptation, regret, anger, jealousy, worry, and fear can easily take hold. No wonder God tells us to protect our heads with the helmet of salvation (Ephesians 6:17).

Helmets protect the head, which holds the brain, where your mind resides. What's on your head? What's on your mind?

Remembering our salvation is our defense against the enemy of our souls and the father of lies, Satan. He tempts us to question God, just as he tempted Eve in the garden and Jesus in the wilderness. He can't take our salvation away. But he can throw us off balance and make us ineffective by planting seeds of doubt regarding God's love, His forgiveness, and His amazing gift of salvation.

In Matthew 22:37, Jesus said the greatest commandment is to love the Lord your God with all your heart, soul, and mind. How can we love and honor our heavenly Father if our minds are full of spiritual weeds and garbage?

Even if we are wearing every other piece of armor, without the helmet of salvation, we are vulnerable to spiritual attack, leaving us helpless and defeated.

When I get my feelings hurt, I throw myself a well-deserved (or so I think) pity party. I focus on my wants and needs. I want a little more attention and appreciation.

Then I picture my heavenly Father gently shaking His head and saying, *Oh, little one, look at Me. See how much I love you and all I have given you. Rejoice in your salvation. Adjust your helmet, Dyann. Get your mind right and let's go!*

Cognitive neuroscientist Dr. Caroline Leaf, in her book *Switch on Your Brain,* states:

Thoughts are real, physical things that occupy mental real estate. Moment by moment, every day, you are changing the structure of your brain through your thinking. When we hope, it is an activity of the mind that changes the structure of our brain in a positive and normal direction.[2] The process of thinking and choosing is the most powerful thing in the universe after God, and it is a phenomenal gift from God to be treasured and used properly.[3]

---

[2] Leaf, "Switch on Your Brain", 19
[3] Leaf, "Switch on Your Brain", 103

Dr. Leaf's conclusions are not new. God's Word tells us the same thing when we:

- Present our bodies "as a living and holy sacrifice, acceptable to God," and choose not to be "conformed to this world" but to be "transformed" by the renewing of our minds. In doing so, we "prove what the will of God is, that which is good and acceptable and perfect." (See Romans 12:1–2)

- Give our worries to God through prayer with thanksgiving, to guard our hearts and minds. (See Philippians 4:6–7)

- Take "every thought captive to the obedience of Christ," to destroy speculations and lofty things raised against the knowledge of God. (See 2 Corinthians 10:5)

- Dwell on things that are true, honorable, right, pure, lovely, commendable, things that are excellent or praiseworthy, to protect and redirect the spiritual nature of our brains. (See Philippians 4:8)

Each time we make these choices, we are building healthy spiritual habits.

When someone we love heads out of the house to ride a bike, skateboard, motorcycle, or participate in another dangerous activity, we give the standard warning, "Don't forget your helmet!" God says the same thing to us. *Get your mind right by putting on My helmet of salvation. It will protect you from spiritual brain damage.*

Don't forget your helmet today.

Personal Reflection

- How can I remember each day to put on God's helmet of salvation?

- What Scripture verse will I memorize to keep my mind protected?

- Is the Lord prompting me to take a specific step today to renew my mind?

Prayer

Today, Lord, remind me that you are the God of my salvation and my strength. Thank You for providing all the armor I need for a strong spiritual life. Remind me whenever I forget to put on the helmet of salvation. You gave it to me for your protection over my spiritual mind. Amen.

Scripture for Meditation

For the mind set on the flesh is death, but the mind set on the Spirit is life and peace. (Romans 8:6)

For God has not given us a spirit of fear, but of power and of love and

of a sound mind. (2 Timothy 1:7 NKJV)

Saying Goodbye

They will no longer hunger nor thirst,
nor will the sun beat down on them,
nor any scorching heat;
for the Lamb in the center of the throne
will be their shepherd,
and will guide them to springs of the water of life;
and God will wipe every tear from their eyes.
(Revelation 7:16–17)

Saying Goodbye

"See you on the other side, Sis," my brother, Randy, said as we held each other, crying. We knew we probably wouldn't see each other again this side of heaven. Letting go of him was heartbreaking. I wanted to keep him a little longer. A few days later, my brother entered eternity with a new body, no pain, no sorrow, and in the presence of his Lord. It was January and starting the new year with such profound loss was strange for me.

Randy and I were five years apart and had opposite approaches to life. He was the "scrapper" who couldn't be pushed around. I was the older sister, the "pleaser," who wanted to avoid confrontation. "Live under the radar so no one would notice" was my unspoken motto.

We grew up in a neighborhood filled with children whose fathers had returned from World War II, many with physical and emotional injuries. They were hard-working men trying to get back to normal. Our dad grew up during the Great Depression. His family moved from town to town as his father looked for work. Dad moved west at seventeen after graduating from a small high school in a tiny coal-mining town. He educated himself and worked constantly to ensure he would never be poor or hungry again. Our mother, an only child, was one of the lucky few whose father always had a good job. Fear of poverty was unknown to her.

With Dad working a lot and Mom having medical issues, my brother and I often had to fend for ourselves. We fought over everything: TV, food, control. I am embarrassed now when I remember all those fights.

Randy turned to drugs and alcohol at a young age, and for many years, we rarely saw each other. He struggled with addiction until he was forty-eight, when he got clean and sober. I was so proud of him. He returned to school, made the dean's list, and started a successful business. It was a gift to have him for twenty years more than I ever expected.

My brother used to say, "We're all so broken, Sis," and he was right. We are fragmented people saved by Jesus, who holds us in His mighty hand. He redeems and loves us in our shattered mess. However large or small, when we offer our messy, broken lives to God, He heals and transforms us. My brother was proof that no matter how fractured we are or appear to be, it's never too late to be renewed and restored.

On my last day, as I was leaving to visit Randy at his home, there was a drug incident at the hotel where I was staying. It triggered past fears of one day receiving a call that my brother had died of an overdose. Completely unnerved, I dissolved in an uncontrollable puddle of tears. I could not stop crying. Wanting to regain my composure, I decided to take a brisk walk in the old section of town.

Eventually, I stopped for coffee at a local gathering spot. As I walked in, beautiful praise music filled my ears. Peace enveloped me, joy filled my heart, and my tears ceased. It was a sweet reminder that God is near the brokenhearted. I pivoted from past fears of losing Randy too soon to the current assurance of knowing he was about to be welcomed into eternity by God, our Father.

Letting go of loved ones is agonizing. Even knowing we will spend eternity with them, the human loss is enormous. My brother had two types of rare cancer. He was in pain and reduced to just bones with a thin layer of skin. But as he neared the end of his earthly life, there was a sweetness to the privilege of being with him. I read his favorite Scriptures. I was thrilled when he asked me to pray for him. We hugged and kissed each other more than ever. It was a blessing to massage his feet and rock him in his wheelchair.

Randy did funny things during his last few weeks, like wanting to eat sushi, which he had always called "yesterday's leftover bait." The night before he died, he wanted food from In-N-Out Burger. It was a precious time.

I witnessed the loving care of his sons, his congregation, and his friend David, who frequently transferred him from bed to wheelchair to the bathroom and back. These were priceless gifts.

Kintsugi is a Japanese technique for repairing ceramics with lacquer and a metal powder, gold or silver.[4] This process highlights the brokenness instead of hiding it. Our God does the same with us. He works with and through our brokenness. He takes the cracks, scars,

---

[4]Kintsugi | History, Pottery, & Facts | Britannica

and pieces of our lives and binds them together into something more beautiful and with greater purpose.

In the hand of God, our redeemed imperfection becomes a tool to comfort and encourage others. I love this about the Lord.

The morning Randy died, the daily devotion from his congregation was Ecclesiastes 3:1. "For everything, there is a season, a time for every activity under heaven. A time to be born and a time to die." An hour later, my brother entered the gates of heaven. My heart was sorrowful but grateful.

Personal Reflection

- What brokenness do I need to acknowledge?

- What imperfection can I offer to the Lord to shine through today?

- What loss do I need to grieve and let go?

Prayer

Today, Lord, thank you for shining through my imperfections. When I turn my brokenness over to You, You use it to comfort, encourage, and minister to others. Help me allow the perfection of Jesus to shine through my imperfection. Amen.

Scripture for Meditation

On one of our last days together, Randy asked me to read his favorite Scriptures, **Psalm 139** and **Psalm 51**. I encourage you to read these Psalms along with the Scriptures below for your meditation.

This light momentary affliction is preparing for us an eternal weight of glory beyond all comparison, as we look not to the things that are seen but to the things that are unseen. For the things that are seen are transient, but the things that are unseen are eternal. (2 Corinthians 4:17-18 ESV)

To me, to live is Christ, and to die is gain. But if I am to live on in the flesh, this will mean fruitful labor for me; and I do not know which to choose. But I am hard-pressed from both directions, having the desire to depart and be with Christ, for that is very much better. (Philippians 1:21–23)

Privilege of Prayer

Be anxious for nothing, but in everything
by prayer and supplication with thanksgiving
let your requests be made known to God.
And the peace of God,
which surpasses all comprehension,
will guard your hearts and your minds in Christ Jesus.
(Philippians 4:6–7)

Privilege of Prayer

Do you ever feel a sense of sadness or grief, but you don't know why? Does your heart sometimes hurt deeply over a news story, a tragedy in your life, an illness or loss, and you feel so helpless and overwhelmed that you don't have the words to express your pain? In times like those, you may not even know how or what to pray.

Prayer is the lifeline of our communication with God. Jesus gave us the Lord's Prayer as a model (Matthew 6:9-13). Many books and sermons have suggested various tools to enhance our prayer life, such as "ACTS: Adoration, Confession, Thanksgiving, and Supplication."

I usually start my prayers with adoration. But too often, I move quickly into supplication. I know God understands this about me, and I don't think He minds. After all, David, who was called "a man after God's own heart" (1 Samuel 13:14), often began his prayers by praising God but soon begged God to help him overcome a problem.

Fortunately, God is not judging our prayers. He looks at the intent of our hearts. In Psalm 51:17 (NKJV), David declared, "The sacrifices of God are a broken spirit, a broken and a contrite heart—these, O God, You will not despise."

Scripture tells us to pray without ceasing (1 Thessalonians 5:17), pray about everything with thanksgiving (Philippians 4:6), pray sacrificially (Hebrews 13:15), and pray faithfully (Romans 12:12). There is power in prayer. There is also purpose in prayer. It transforms our minds, guards our hearts, and reveals God's purposes in our lives. It is an act of worship and an act of obedience. As believers, prayer is our responsibility, our right, and our privilege.

Prayer is one of the greatest gifts God has given us. The Creator of the universe allows us, in ways we cannot understand, to work with Him on behalf of others and ourselves through prayer. He lets us participate in His divine nature: to tap into the power, the glory, the mind, the love, the peace, and the wisdom of God. This truth is worthy of praise and deep reflection. I don't understand how it works, but I know it to be true.

When communicating with friends, children, or our spouses, we often ponder just the right word or phrase before we speak or write, in order to be heard and understood. But with God, whether we pray audibly or silently, our words don't have to be perfect, because He knows our thoughts.

He hears us even when we don't speak out loud. He understands us even when we don't understand ourselves. We can turn over our words and prayers to the Holy Spirit, who will intercede for us with groanings too deep for words (Romans 8:26).

This reality is a great comfort to me. I have the privilege of pouring out my heart to the Lord. He hears me. He accepts me just as I am, with no pretenses. Through prayer comes the peace that passes all understanding (Philippians 4:7), that quiet assurance that all is or will be well with my soul.

We don't have to be extraordinary to pray. Prayer is available to young and old, healthy and ill, saint and sinner. Jesus is always available, anytime and anywhere. Psalm 121:3 says, "He who watches over you will not slumber."

We may not get the response to prayer that we want, or even an acceptable alternative. God's answer may be "no" or "not now." However, we can trust that His response to our prayers is always for our good and in our best interests.

Some of the simplest and purest prayers are "Not my will but Your will be done" (Luke 22:42) and "I believe; help me in my unbelief" (Mark 9:24). Sometimes our most heartfelt prayer is simply "Help me, Lord."

Whether you are in a time of adoration or supplication, God hears your prayers. And He receives them with joy and acceptance. He is always ready to comfort you. Wherever you are, He is there. Rest in this assurance, and be blessed!

- What keeps me from turning to God in prayer?

- Is there an attitude, a habit, or a sin I need to leave on the altar before God?

- What is one thing I can offer as praise to God today?

Today, Lord, I give you thanks for hearing my prayers. You are my loving Father. You know my heart. You understand my weaknesses, my intent, my hurts, and my sorrows. Whether my prayer is a simple "Help" or an eloquent expression of praise, You hear and know my voice. Thank You. Amen.

Grace and peace be multiplied to you in the knowledge of God and of Jesus our Lord, for His divine power has granted to us everything pertaining to life and godliness, through the true knowledge of Him who called us by His own glory and excellence. Through these He has granted to us His precious and magnificent promises, so that by them you may become partakers of the divine nature, having escaped the corruption that is in the world on account of lust. (2 Peter 1:2–4)

I heard a loud voice from the throne saying, "Look! God's dwelling place is now among the people, and he will dwell with them. They will be his people, and God himself will be with them and be their God. 'He will wipe every tear from their eyes. There will be no more death' or mourning or crying or pain, for the old order of things has passed away." (Revelation 21:3–4 NIV)

Prayer as Preparation

My soul, wait silently for God alone,

for my expectation is from Him.

He only is my rock and my salvation;

He is my defense; I shall not be moved.

In God is my salvation and my glory;

the rock of my strength, and my refuge, is in God.

Trust in Him at all times, you people;

pour out your heart before Him;

God is a refuge for us.

(Psalm 62:5–8 NKJV)

Prayer as Preparation

Sometimes God puts something on our hearts to prepare us for a future need.

As I was writing a blog post about "The Privilege of Prayer," I prayed for my future readers. I prayed that my writing would meet at least one person's needs.

It never occurred to me that the person in need would be me.

I finalized my blog post and set it for release the following day. That night, I received a call from my youngest son, Jonathan. He was ill with extreme stomach pain and had lost forty pounds during the previous month. I spent a long time on the phone talking and praying with him.

When my blog came out the next morning, Jonathan called and said, "Mom, I know you wrote today's blog post before last night. But it was exactly what we talked and prayed about on the phone."

I had prayed that my writing would touch at least one person. And God answered my prayer. My blog was for my son and for me. We both realized that God had put that topic on my heart weeks before to prepare us for this moment.

Later that day, Jonathan was admitted to the hospital. I hoped he would be home in a few hours with a straightforward diagnosis and treatment plan. But that didn't happen.

I booked a flight right away to be with him in the hospital. It was a long week, filled with prayer, tears, anxious thoughts, and fear. My son was often heavily medicated, so our conversations were short. While he had tests and procedures, I took walks and prayed on the trails and alongside the river behind the hospital. The beauty of God's creation provided the peace I needed as each test came back without a diagnosis.

Occasionally, a nurse, a doctor, or the hospital chaplain came in and talked with us. Sometimes Jonathan's pastor or neighbor dropped by. Each person was a reminder that we were not alone.

As I gazed at my son, weak and frail, I reminded myself that I had always said my children were on loan to me from God. Jonathan was God's child before he was mine. I needed this assurance while we lived in the season of "unknown" answers.

Years ago, a wise friend advised me to "pray ahead" for my children. I had made this a lifelong practice. Words for prayer often escaped me as I sat by Jonathan's bed. But I was grateful for the prayers I had stored up on his behalf. And God knew my heart.

Job 33:4 (NKJV) says, "The Spirit of God has made me, and the breath of the Almighty gives me life." And in Acts 17:28 (NKJV), we are told that we are God's creation. "In Him, we live and move and have our being." These are powerful statements. The Bible tells us to write the Word of God on our hearts, pray, and show love, joy, faithfulness, peace, and gratitude (Deuteronomy 6:6-7, 11:18, Proverbs 3:3). By memorizing and practicing scripture we build our spiritual endurance. Runners do not decide to run a marathon on the day of the race. They prepare. And so must we.

The walk of faith often feels perilous. We don't know what the next day or the next phone call will present. Life is often accompanied by twists, turns, curves, and sometimes road closures. Prayer and worship help us to stay close to God and prepare us for these unexpected seasons. Just as birds store food for the winter, we must store up prayers.

By praying ahead for our children, our family, and life in general, we prepare ourselves for the marathon of life. When the moment of need comes, our response will be determined by the amount of God's Word we have consumed, prayed about, and applied to our daily lives.

If we are too overwhelmed to pray, we can ask others to pray on our behalf.

The answers to my prayers for Jonathan's complete healing were not what I had hoped for, but there has been improvement. He is still in pain but back at work. There are certain foods he can't tolerate. We still don't have a definitive diagnosis. This season has been challenging. But life is messy. We want it neat, well defined, and controllable. But if there were never uncertainty, we wouldn't need to trust. We wouldn't see God's power and provision, or experience His peace in our circumstances.

In the chaos of life, we experience God's love, comfort, strength, and hope when we exercise our faith.

I don't know what the future holds. But I do know God holds my future and my son's future. That is enough.

I hope you know God loves you. I pray that you are entrusting your future to Him.

Personal Reflection

- Who or what in my life can I give to God by "praying ahead"?

- What uncertain situation in my life can I give to God?

- What will I implement in my spiritual life today to build the practice of prayer?

Prayer

Today, Lord, I am grateful that you are with me in the messiness of life. Please help me to turn to You in the hard places more quickly. Thank You for forgiving me when I try to solve my problems alone. Amen.

Scripture for Meditation

Now faith is the assurance of things hoped for, the conviction of things not seen. (Hebrews 11:1 ESV)

Pray in the Spirit on all occasions with all kinds of prayers and requests. With this in mind, be alert and always keep on praying for all the Lord's people. (Ephesians 6:18 NIV)

My soul, wait silently for God alone, for my expectation is from Him.

He only is my rock and my salvation; He is my defense; I shall not be moved.

In God is my salvation and my glory; the rock of my strength, and my refuge, is in God.

Trust in Him at all times, you people; pour out your heart before Him; God is a refuge for us. (Psalm 62:5–8 NKJV)

Can Grief and Gratitude Coexist?

Cast all your anxiety on him
because he cares for you.
(1 Peter 5:7 NIV)

Can Grief and Gratitude Coexist?

"My brain doesn't work," my husband, Rick, announced as he was waking up. "What?" I responded. Again, my husband said, "My brain doesn't work!" That morning, there was a sudden and dramatic decline in his cognitive abilities. He was completely lost and confused. And so, we began the final eight months of his earthly life. Within two weeks, he couldn't drive, work out at the gym, or play bridge.

For several years, we had been on the Alzheimer's journey. Rick was forgetful and occasionally unable to perform a simple task. It was challenging but manageable. The process was like watching a cliff toss off rocks in bits and pieces. But on December 1, 2023, there was a seismic shift similar to a landslide. Rick's brain was changed forever. We were in shock over his decline. His doctor prescribed medications but nothing worked. His helplessness filled him with fear.

I felt helpless too. I prayed, *Lord, I don't know what to do. I don't know how to help him. Show me the way!*

Not audibly, but clear nonetheless, *I am the Way, Dyann. Keep your eyes on Me. I will guide you. I will show you the way.*

Further along as I tried to help Rick, he kept saying "No" or "I can't." I felt overwhelmed and I cried out to God praying, *Lord I can't hear "No" or "I can't" one more time.* Again, not audibly but still clear, *Dyann, you're not really listening to your husband. Pay attention to the other things he is saying besides "No" and "I can't." Change the filter of your ears.*

When I really listened, I realized Rick was saying many other things to me: "Sweetie, I love you. Thank you. I just want to take care of you. You look beautiful today." I would have missed those tender words if I hadn't changed my focus. I wrote them in my journal, not wanting to forget them.

Grief and loss filled the next few months, but in the midst, I also felt deep love and gratitude. I experienced Rick's devotion to me as he tried to express himself. My love for him deepened as I served him, which was an unexpected and wonderful gift. I gained a more profound appreciation for God's provision as I journaled my pain, fear, exhaustion, and requests.

Watching your loved one die is lonely and heartbreaking. But in the quiet of loneliness, there is a unique opportunity to draw near to God and cling to Him. His presence was with me and my husband throughout the journey as I poured out our needs and pain in lament.

During the last months of Rick's life on earth, my eyes could not focus on the words in my Bible.

So, I listened to Scripture on my phone. As exhaustion took over, I struggled to pray, but I trusted the Holy Spirit to intercede for me with groanings too deep for words (Romans 8:26).

My dear Rick entered eternity in July of 2024. Revisiting my journals afterward, I reflected on all God had provided: loving caregivers, cards of encouragement, friends who dropped by with meals or to visit and pray.

Most importantly, I praised God for the peace Rick experienced as he left his physical body.

Beloved friend, whatever your struggle, pour out your heart to your heavenly Father. He loves you and promised never to leave you or forsake you (Deuteronomy 31:8). Let Him do fresh work in the weeds of your pain. He is with you and a very present help in trouble (Psalm 46:1). There is no reason to withhold your longings.

At the same time, ask the Lord to open your eyes and ears to His goodness. I encourage you to journal your laments, longings, and thankfulness.

Yes, grief and gratitude can coexist if you allow them to live together. Psalm 66:16–17 (ESV) says, "Come and hear, all you who fear God, and I will tell what he has done for my soul. I cried to him with my mouth, and high praise was on my tongue."

Amid my loss and grief, I am filled with gratitude for thirty-one years with a kind and loving husband.

Personal Reflection

- What pain or grief can I take to God?

- How am I developing the practice of offering a sacrifice of thanksgiving to the Lord in the midst of my struggle?

- What trusted friends will I invite to help me bear my burden?

Prayer

Today, Lord, I give You praise for the privilege of laying all my troubles at the foot of the cross. You are fully aware of my pain and heartache. I praise You for lighting my path, one step at a time. Your Word says You store my tears in a bottle (Psalm 56:8). Thank You for the promise that You will never leave or forsake me. I will trust You with my future. Amen.

Scripture for Meditation

Likewise, the Spirit helps us in our weakness. For we do not know what to pray for as we ought, but the Spirit himself intercedes for us with groanings too deep for words. (Romans 8:26 ESV)

I will offer to you the sacrifice of thanksgiving and call on the name

of the Lord. (Psalm 116:17 ESV)

Via Dolorosa

Looking only at Jesus,

the originator and perfecter of the faith,

who for the joy set before Him endured the cross,

despising the shame, and has sat down

at the right hand of the throne of God.

(Hebrews 12:2)

Via Dolorosa

The processional to Jerusalem began triumphantly. Excitement filled the air. People laid garments and palm branches on the road like a royal carpet as they praised God with loud, joyful voices declaring, "Blessed is the King who comes in the name of the Lord! Peace in heaven and glory in the highest!" (Luke 19:37–38 NKJV). What an entrance, so full of promise.

Yet by the end of the week, the one the people welcomed and pronounced as King was deserted by all. He was despised, rejected, hung on a cross, killed, and placed in an unmarked tomb as an outcast. He appeared defeated and without hope.

But God … two words that intervened and changed life's trajectory. Three days later, the tomb was empty. The Messiah was not dead but *alive*! He had risen from the grave!

At times, our lives become a journey filled with disappointment, despair, or dilemma. We ask, "Is there another way?"

How hard it is to surrender, as Jesus did, to "not my will but Yours be done."

Are you walking a Via Dolorosa? You are not alone. Jesus is with you. Hebrews 12:1–3 (NKJV) says:

We also, since we are surrounded by so great a cloud of witnesses, let us lay aside every weight, and the sin which so easily ensnares us, and let us run with endurance the race that is set before us, looking unto Jesus, the author and finisher of our faith, who for the joy that was set before Him endured the cross, despising the shame, and has sat down at the right hand of the throne of God.

We often can't fathom how our circumstances could possibly pivot from pain to purpose, from refuse to renewal, restoration, and resurrection. But God has shown us the way through Jesus, who endured His Via Dolorosa for you and for me.

Beloved,

- Fix your eyes on Jesus (Hebrews 12:2)
- Anchor your soul to Him (Hebrews 6:19)

- Hold fast the confession of your faith (Hebrews 10:23)

- Never let Him go, for He is your peace and life (John 14:6, 27)

Praise Him. He is risen. He is risen indeed.

Personal Reflection

- Am I taking time to reflect on the sacrifice of Jesus?

- Am I praising God regularly for His victory over death on my behalf?

- How am I surrendering my personal Via Dolorosa to Jesus?

Prayer

Today, Lord, I realize there are no words to express the depth of Your love. It is too wonderful for me to comprehend. Thank You for forgiving me when I focus on my personal Via Dolorosa to the extent that I forget yours. You went before me, suffered and died for me. You conquered death so that I could be raised with You in glory. Praise Your holy Name. You only are to be praised. Amen.

Scripture for Meditation

Who, as He already existed in the form of God, did not consider equality with God something to be grasped, but emptied Himself by taking the form of a bond-servant and being born in the likeness of men. And being found in appearance as a man, He humbled Himself by becoming obedient to the point of death: death on a cross. For this reason also God highly exalted Him, and bestowed on Him the name which is above every name, so that at the name of Jesus EVERY KNEE WILL BOW, of those who are in heaven and on earth and under the earth, and that every tongue will confess that Jesus Christ is Lord, to the glory of God the Father. (Philippians 2:6–11)

For this reason I bend my knees before the Father, from whom every family in heaven and on earth derives its name, that He would grant you, according to the riches of His glory, to be strengthened with power through His Spirit in the inner self, so that Christ may dwell in your hearts through faith; and that you, being rooted and grounded in love, may be able to comprehend with all the saints what is the width and length and height and depth, and to know the love of Christ which surpasses knowledge, that you may be filled to all the fullness of God.

Now to Him who is able to do far more abundantly beyond all that we ask or think, according to the power that works within us, to Him be the glory in the church and in Christ Jesus to all generations forever and ever. Amen. (Ephesians 3:14–21)

Transformations

I urge you, brothers and sisters,

in view of God's mercy,

to offer your bodies as a living sacrifice,

holy and pleasing to God—

this is your true and proper worship.

Do not conform to the pattern of this world,

but be transformed by the renewing of your mind.

Then you will be able to test and approve

what God's will is—

his good, pleasing and perfect will.

(Romans 12:1–2 NIV)

Transformations

The Apostle Paul's urging in Romans 12:1–2 is a call to action: to be transformed, to have a renewed mind. I want my life to reflect God's good, pleasing, and perfect will. It is an admirable goal. But it's challenging. It requires relinquishing control. Change happens from the inside out, and it takes time. God's time.

Recently, I struggled with an outer change I knew I needed. I'd been coloring my hair for a long time, but finally, I decided it was time to go *au natural*. This was a long process. Every day, I looked in the mirror and saw more strands of neon white hair taking over. I often wanted to give up and return to the old me.

For months, I had what appeared to be a brown beanie on my head. Several times, I thought, *Forget it. This is too hard, it takes too long, and I look too old.* I wanted to go back to what was familiar.

But isn't that the way we are spiritually? We want God to transform us into the image of Jesus, but we don't want to go through the process. It's uncomfortable, it's painful, and it takes too long. We want a shortcut.

But there are no shortcuts to godliness.

Thankfully, God is patient with us as He teaches us patience. He is gentle with us as He teaches us gentleness. He forgives us in order to teach us true forgiveness. He is full of unconditional love, teaching us how to give unconditional love.

When we first trusted Jesus for our salvation, God created a new person. He wants us to experience our new life through the transformative power of the Holy Spirit. This begins with an internal change.

But outer changes are much more manageable. It's easy to change our hair color or clothing style. If we're determined, we can lose weight. But inner change means letting go of our perceived rights, our control and yielding to the work of the Holy Spirit.

Spiritual change usually comes through trials and struggles. Our transformation can be compared to that of a caterpillar becoming a butterfly.

A caterpillar crawls on stems and leaves, happily going about its little life. When it attaches itself to the proper source, it slowly becomes wrapped up in a chrysalis, which leads to a total change from the inside out.

There is no rushing metamorphosis. The struggle of pushing through the chrysalis releases the fluids necessary to strengthen the caterpillar's new wings. It cannot fly if it does not go through the complete process. At the proper time, the caterpillar pushes through the chrysalis, revealing the transformation. The crawling insect is now a soaring butterfly.

As believers, we often act like the caterpillar, crawling through life, seeing only what is directly before us. But God's plan is for us to soar. To become what we are meant to be, we must be transformed.

Our inner renewal begins when we surrender to the Holy Spirit and allow Him to reveal those areas where we are crawling. When we turn those things over to the Lord, yielding them to Jesus, we begin to become the new creatures we are in Christ. Paul calls it putting on "the new man" (Ephesians 4:24).

We must choose to allow God to use the struggles and pressures of life in order to produce in us His glory. Praise God, His ways are not our ways. Our way almost always involves taking the easy path. He says, "No, my child. The difficult path is longer, but it is where you will grow the most. I want your spiritual wings to be strong so you can soar above your circumstances."

Always remember, Jesus loves you, is for you, and is with you as you are being transformed into His image.

Personal Reflection

- What changes am I resisting?

- Where am I trying to shortcut my spiritual growth?

- What areas of my life have I held back from surrendering to the Holy Spirit?

Prayer

Today, Lord, I thank You for Your gentle patience and love for me even when I resist You. Please help me yield to Your Holy Spirit to be transformed from the inside out. Reveal the areas that I hold back and give me a heart of surrender to grow in faith and renew my mind. I want to be like Jesus. Amen.

Scripture for Meditation

If any man be in Christ, he is a new creature: old things are passed away; behold, all things are become new. (2 Corinthians 5:17 KJV)

After you have suffered a little while, the God of all grace, who has

called you to his eternal glory in Christ, will himself restore, confirm,

strengthen, and establish you. (1 Peter 5:10 ESV)

Imprisoned Without Bars

For God has not given us a spirit of fear,

but of power and of love and of a sound mind.

(2 Timothy 1:7 NKJV)

Most of us have people whose lives have made lasting impressions on us. Two of these in my life were my sweet grandma and my dear friend, Steve.

My grandma led a simple, somewhat sheltered life. She wasn't well educated, but her life shone brightly with the love of God. Her example and prayers led me to faith in Jesus. Her sweet spirit calmed me in the midst of a difficult childhood.

My dear friend, Steve, had MS. He spent his days reading his Bible and praying. He had the glow of Jesus on his face. Love and joy poured out from him. The caretakers at the facility where he lived often asked him for prayer. Steve sent an encouraging Bible verse to his close friends every morning. I was blessed to be in that special circle. He had a tiny corner of the world to tend to, but the fruit of that plot was plentiful.

Both my grandmother, who never learned to drive, and my friend, Steve, confined to a nursing home, experienced "sheltering in place" long before it became a household phrase during the COVID-19 pandemic and civil unrest. Despite their circumstances, both continued to encourage and bless others with their love and kindness. They were content and at peace.

With or without pandemics, protests, or personal upheaval, we are each faced with the question of how we will respond when we experience an unexpected and unwanted change. Will our lives reflect fear and despair or trust and hope?

Recently, I began reflecting on how much time and energy I waste on fear and worry. I hide behind palatable terms like *concern* or *anticipation*. The truth is, these words make me feel better about my anxiety and fearfulness.

As I study Scripture, I notice words like *captive* or being *entangled*: words that describe restrained movement, a lack of freedom, or a lack of forward momentum. I wonder how much of my life is spent in this self-imposed confinement that keeps me from being useful, peaceful, and the person God created me to be. This prison does not have bars of steel but of trepidation and uncertainty. I am like the servant whose master gave him one talent, and instead of investing it, he hid it out of fear of losing it.

When reports of another protest, school shooting, assassination, or war fills the news, we are reminded of how much of life is out of our control. But we can control our response. We have a unique opportunity to ask the Lord where we can shine His light of love, hope, encouragement, and provision to those less fortunate.

Times of uncertainty are also times of opportunity to discover who we really are and what our character is. Are we hoarders or givers? Will we withhold love and compassion, or will we look for areas to help, love, encourage, and supply? Will we offer a sacrifice of praise and thanksgiving to our God or complain about all we don't have or might lose? It is a moment-by-moment choice.

God has provided each of us with something to give in unplanned seasons of disruption and change. Our gift may meet a financial, spiritual, emotional, or physical need. As I pray for those who are suffering, I also pray for wisdom and insight into new and creative ways to reach out. I want to learn to step out of my physical or emotional confinement to help, even if I must remain at home.

"Now may our Lord Jesus Christ Himself and God our Father, who has loved us and given us eternal comfort and good hope by grace, comfort and strengthen your hearts in every good work and word." (2 Thessalonians 2:16–17)

Personal Reflection

- Is there a friend I can bless with a call or visit to remind them they are not forgotten?

- Am I thanking God regularly for what I do have and can do rather than focusing on what I can't do and don't have?

- Will I take time today to rest in God's presence?

Prayer

Today, Lord, enlarge my heart to look past my personal fears and find opportunities to see and meet the needs of others. Forgive me for imprisoning myself due to anxiety and discontent. Help me release these invisible bars that keep me from experiencing Your love, power, and strength. Amen.

Scripture for Meditation

Do not be anxious about anything, but in every situation, by prayer and petition, with thanksgiving, present your requests to God. And the peace of God, which transcends all understanding, will guard your

hearts and your minds in Christ Jesus. (Philippians 4:6-7 NIV)

I shall run the way of Your commandments, for You will enlarge my

heart. (Psalm 119:32)

Cleaning Our Spiritual Filters

Who can understand his errors?

Cleanse me from secret faults.

(Psalm 19:12 NKJV)

Cleaning Our Spiritual Filters

Usually, when I clean the filter of my clothes dryer, I merely pick out the small loose fibers. But recently I pulled out the entire filter and was shocked at all the packed-in lint. There was no doubt my dryer had been working overtime. It made me wonder, "What kind of spiritual gunk am I accumulating and therefore slowing down the work of the Holy Spirit in my life?"

I have learned that physical clutter is usually a sign of spiritual clutter in my life. When I look around my office or home and see only piles, I have probably pulled back control from the Holy Spirit. I feel overwhelmed. I don't know where to begin to put order back into my spiritual and physical life.

I need to stop, take a deep breath, pray, and allow God to reveal what I need to deal with—beyond the obvious of putting papers in the proper file or hanging up my clothes. It's time to ask what spiritual issues need to be addressed and, more importantly, to listen. It is not a pleasant process, but it is a freeing one.

Giving and asking for forgiveness are my most vulnerable areas for accumulating spiritual clutter. This trait saddens me because, truth be told, I am stingy with forgiveness and confession. I tend to excuse myself for what seems to me to be insignificant and minor infractions, like a snippy response to my husband when I'm tired. *No big deal*, I tell myself. But it is.

Each time I fail to confess and ask for forgiveness, a type of spiritual plaque builds up. The free flow of God's Spirit is inhibited, like the buildup of lint in my dryer or bad cholesterol in my arteries. Eventually, I risk not hearing God's gentle prompting to apologize.

Jesus reminds us in Luke 16:10, "The one who is faithful in a very little thing is also faithful in much; and the one who is unrighteous in a very little thing is also unrighteous in much." Whenever I ignore the Lord's conviction in a minor matter, I risk falling into sin in a significant matter, progressively searing my conscience.

The beautiful truth is that my Father knows my weaknesses. He provided His Son's sacrifice for them. And the way to daily cleanse my spiritual filter is confession: the acknowledgment of wrongdoing. The Amplified Bible expresses our need for confession this way in James 5:16: "Confess your sins to one another [your false steps, your offenses], and pray for one another, that you may be healed and restored. The heartfelt and persistent prayer of a righteous man (believer) can accomplish much [when put into action and made effective by God—it is dynamic and can have tremendous power]."

Confession is not for God's sake but for ours. The Lord knows that as we acknowledge our offenses, we keep our relationship with Him and others healthy. When we practice admitting wrongdoing, we build spiritual muscle memory, making confession easier and more automatic.

When I confess my sins, I feel freer. In this intentional act of giving up my pride, there is a sense of refreshment and renewal as I allow the fruit of the Spirit to grow and thrive in me.

It's time for spring cleaning. Won't you join me by letting go of any accumulated spiritual lint and the clutter of old hurts, unforgiveness, disappointments, and pride? Make room for all that

God has provided. He has given us free access to His lavish and nonperishable gifts of love, joy, peace, and forgiveness.

Personal Reflection

- What spiritual clutter have I allowed to build up in my life?

- Is there anyone I need to ask for forgiveness?

- What am I intentionally doing to keep spiritual lint from accumulating?

Prayer

Today, Lord, please reveal to me the areas of spiritual clutter in my life You want me to confess. Please give me the courage to acknowledge my sin and forsake it in order to keep spiritual lint from building up in my life. Please give me the strength to ask for forgiveness regardless of how insignificant the offense may seem to me. Thank you for forgiving me. Amen.

Scripture for Meditation

Search me, God, and know my heart; put me to the test and know my anxious thoughts; and see if there is any hurtful way in me, and lead me in an everlasting way. (Psalm 139:23–24)

Be kind to one another, tenderhearted, forgiving one another, even as

God in Christ forgave you. (Ephesians 4:32 NKJV)

Life Lessons from Spiritual Fracking

I will give you a new heart

and put a new spirit in you;

I will remove from you your heart of stone

and give you a heart of flesh.

(Ezekiel 36:26 NIV)

When my boys were young, I often told them, "Keep your spirit strong but your heart soft." Little did I know my own heart had become hard.

The revelation began when our church announced a meeting on fracking. I was familiar with the term because my brother was driving fracking equipment at the time. According to him, the fracking process involves drilling a deep tunnel into the ground and shooting hot water and chemicals down the hole with tremendous pressure to release the oil and gas from the solid oil shale.

My husband and I attended the meeting. In a monotone voice, the speaker read from her notes about the consequences of fracking. When some members of the audience questioned her conclusions, she seemed dismissive and defensive. Even rude. With feelings of anger building inside me, I raised my hand.

"Do you have a question?" she asked.

"No," I said, "I have a comment. I would appreciate it if you would give the same respect to the audience that we have given you."

The room fell into total silence. My husband looked stunned. I had publicly reprimanded the guest speaker.

When we returned home, I felt confused by my behavior. I couldn't remember ever feeling so much inner turmoil. Why had I gotten so mad? I felt ashamed for being so rude.

To make matters worse, I had just finished an in-depth study of the book of Proverbs regarding the effect of our words.

During the next few weeks, I prayed, cried, and had honest discussions with the women in my Bible study. I eventually realized the feelings I had for the guest speaker were the same ones I'd felt long ago when my mother cut people off or disregarded their point of view, which was a common occurrence in our home and at social gatherings. Those situations embarrassed me, and I felt angry when she was disrespectful.

As the Lord revealed the root cause of my anger, I realized I had just been "fracked." My heart was hard and needed the extreme pressure of embarrassment and shame to break up the hardness. The hot pressure of God's Spirit broke up old hurts and brought them to the surface. Scars from my childhood and the hard rock of my heart were revealed. I laughed at the ironic humor. I'd thought I was going to a meeting on oil shale fracking, but the Lord had other "fracking" to do.

I called the person at church who had arranged the meeting and apologized. When I offered to call the speaker, she said it wasn't necessary, and I gratefully accepted the "pass." However, as the years went by, I was never at peace about the incident. I'd had my "fracking moment" and understood where my reaction came from, but I hadn't completed the process. I needed to ask for forgiveness from the speaker.

Three years later, I tracked the speaker down. I emailed her and asked if we could meet. I didn't tell her why, only that I had heard her speak at our church. Driving to our appointment, I prayed, "Lord, how should I approach this? What do I say?" I felt His gentle nudge. *Spend time getting to know her, and listen.*

She didn't recognize me, but welcomed me with a warm smile as I introduced myself. When I asked how she had gotten involved in the anti-fracking movement, she shared her love for the community, the environment, and her concerns as a mother. I told her about my brother's work in the oil fields.

Finally, I said, "The reason I wanted to meet with you is to ask for your forgiveness for being so rude to you that night."

Her eyes filled with tears. She told me it was the first time she had given the presentation. She believed she had failed and cried all the way home.

I told her I was sorry for the pain I had caused. It had nothing to do with her. Issues from my past had surfaced. They were revealed during a Bible study. As emotional scars had been broken up and brought to the surface, I realized I'd been "fracked by God." The experience had become a powerful lesson of how rocklike our hearts can become without our awareness. She laughed at this analogy.

We spent the remainder of our time sharing our experiences as mothers and our desire to impart the essential character qualities of respect and kindness to our children. We spoke as two moms who loved our community and our families.

When we got up to say goodbye, I wanted to hug her, but I wasn't sure how it would be received. She immediately said, "Oh, we have to hug." It was a wonderful time of healing for both of us.

My spiritual fracking was timelier than I realized. Months before that meeting at our church, I had written in my prayer journal a request for genuine compassion for my mother. She was in a nursing home but was still very challenging and demanding. I prayed that before she died, I would have genuine empathy for her as a human being.

To have compassion for my mother, I needed to let go of the child within me—the child whose mom had mental health issues due to a personality disorder. I needed to remember my mother was also God's child. I had forgotten all about that prayer. But during the three years following my spiritual fracking, my heart softened. The duty of seeing my mom turned to compassion.

On the day she died, she had the countenance of an angel: sweet and with a soft glow. I had never seen such a peaceful look on her face. I didn't know it was her final day on earth.

That last memory of her was God's gift to me. My prayer for a softened heart was answered. I was at peace.

Personal Reflection

- Is there a hard place in my heart that needs to be broken up and "fracked"?

- Is there someone I have hurt that I need to ask forgiveness from?

- Am I missing a gift from God because I am unwilling to give up my hurt?

Prayer

Today, Lord, thank You for forgiving my hard heart. Please continue to reveal those areas in my life that are rocklike and damage others as well as myself. Remind me to bring my hurts and confessions to You in order to experience Your healing and grace. Amen.

Scripture for Meditation

If we confess our sins, He is faithful and just to forgive us our sins and to cleanse us from all unrighteousness. (1 John 1:9 NKJV)

Nothing is hidden that will not be made manifest, nor is anything secret that will not be known and come to light. (Luke 8:17 ESV)

What's the Cry of Your Heart?

Behold what manner of love
the Father has bestowed on us,
that we should be called children of God!
Therefore the world does not know us,
because it did not know Him.

(1 John 3:1 NKJV)

What's the Cry of Your Heart?

Recently my prayer has been, "Lord, give me a pure spirit, a pure heart."

It began when I woke up in the middle of the night. Like many of a certain age, sleep for me is rarely uninterrupted. I have learned to use this time for prayer. On this night, the words "Lord, give me a pure spirit" popped into my mind. I knew I would forget my middle-of-the-night prayer by morning, so I wrote down this random thought God had put on my heart and continued my prayers. Eventually, I fell asleep.

In the morning, blurry-eyed and stretching as I roused, I noticed the words scribbled on my notepad: "Lord, give me a pure spirit." I wasn't sure why that prayer came into my mind, so I tucked it away for another day.

A week later, during a Sunday morning children's program, I observed the purity of heart in the little second- and third-graders who sang sweet songs they had practiced and practiced. They stood up straight, forgetting to smile, not wanting to sing the wrong words, as they fixed their eyes on the teacher, who was mouthing the lyrics.

As usual, there was one child who knew every word, every verse, every move. He'd waited eagerly for this moment when he could sing his little heart out for Jesus. Totally into the performance, he belted out the words, singing with abandon, throwing his whole body into the song. His tousled hair flopped up and down and his arms swooped from right to left as he sang, "It is the cry of my heart to follow you all the days of my life." He was pure of spirit and pure of heart.

Just then, I remembered my prayer. "Lord, give me a pure spirit." I wanted to be like that little boy, wholly devoted to Jesus.

After the children finished singing, our pastor presented a new Bible to each one. They all received the gifts with a polite "Thank you." But when the last little girl, in a white frilly dress and black Mary Jane shoes, took her Bible, she opened it, inspected it, and joyfully pressed it to her heart. She received it as the precious, sacred gift it is. She opened it again, touched it reverently, and returned it to her chest as she left for her Sunday school classroom. When she returned to the sanctuary for the benediction, she was still holding her Bible tightly against her chest.

My prayer and the cry of my heart is "Oh Lord, give me a pure spirit like these little children."

God desires us to come to Him with a pure spirit and a heart wholly devoted to Him. In Psalm 119:11, David says, "I have treasured your word in my heart so that I may not sin against you."

That tender moment at church reminds me of the story in Mark 10:13–16 when the disciples rebuked the parents who brought their children to Jesus for Him to touch. But when Jesus saw it, He was indignant and said to them, "Let the children come to me; do not hinder them, for to such belongs the kingdom of God. Truly, I say to you, whoever does not receive the kingdom of God like a child shall not enter it." And He took them in His arms and blessed them, laying His hands on them.

Sometimes I forget to see myself as God's child. I come to Him as an adult, thinking I have all the answers. I forget the endearing names Jesus uses to refer to me: My little child, My beloved, My friend, My daughter.

He sees you that way too. Jesus values us. The cry of His heart is for us to be close to Him, to be in Him as He is in the Father, to be one with Him.

What is the cry of your heart today? Maybe you don't know it or can't express it in words. Yet you feel an undefined longing, an internal need. Ask the Lord to define that hunger.

Picture yourself climbing into the arms of Jesus as a little child seeking to be blessed by Him. Be enveloped by His love, assurance, and tender mercy. Imagine Jesus whispering to you some of the words from Matthew 5:3–12 like "Blessed are you when you are poor in spirit, for I have given you the kingdom of God. Blessed are you when you mourn, I will comfort you or when you hunger and thirst after righteousness, I will satisfy you."

Come as His little child today. Let Psalm 46:10 (ESV) sink in. "Be still, and know that I am God." He is your Abba, your Daddy, your Father. If you need comfort, let Him comfort you. If you need

assurance, let Him reassure you.

Rest in His arms and be refreshed.

Personal Reflection

- Will I take time today to let Jesus hold me as a child?

- Will I pour out my longings to God who loves me?

- Will I "be still and know" and listen for my Father's voice?

Prayer

Today, Lord, I give you thanks for the privilege of coming to You as a child. You say I can call You Abba, Daddy. This blessing is too wonderful for me to comprehend. But as Your child, thank You. Help me, Father, to sit quietly with You, to listen, to be still, and to enjoy Your presence. Amen.

Scripture for Meditation

Try praying the Beatitudes in **Matthew 5:1-12**, using your own name (Blessed are you, _______, when …)

They [the people] were bringing children to Him so that He would touch them; but the disciples rebuked them. But when Jesus saw this,

He was indignant and said to them, "Allow the children to come to Me; do not forbid them, for the kingdom of God belongs to such as these. Truly I say to you, whoever does not receive the kingdom of God like a child will not enter it at all." (Mark 10:13–15)

Is It Possible to Do God's Will but in the Wrong Way?

Do not say to your neighbor,

"Go, and come back,

and tomorrow I will give it to you,"

when you have it with you.

(Proverbs 3:28)

Is It Possible to Do God's Will but in the Wrong Way?

I keep gift cards for food and clothing in my purse to offer when I see people beside the road looking for handouts. If housing is needed, I share the location of our local homeless shelter. After all, cash could be used for alcohol or drugs, which I do not want to fund.

One week after church, a woman who was not part of our congregation, stood outside the sanctuary, asking people for money. When she approached me, I offered her a gift card. She said she wanted money instead. I declined.

The following week, she again waited outside the sanctuary after church. We had the same conversation. I asked if she was hungry. No. Did she need clothes? No. Did she need shelter? No. She needed money for a medical procedure.

Again, not trusting the validity of her request, I declined. But I couldn't stop thinking about her. I felt uncomfortable. *Lord,* I asked, *did I blow it? Did You want me to give her money?*

God reminded me of the parable Jesus told about the Good Samaritan (Luke 10:25–37). The Samaritan didn't ask the beaten man, "What did you do to deserve the beating?" And in Matthew 25:31–46, Jesus didn't imply that someone should interrogate a person in need with questions like "What did you do to end up in prison?" or "Why can't you get your own cup of cold water?" In James 2:14–17, James doesn't suggest that when we see someone without clothes or food, we should ask, "Can't you get a job and buy what you need?"

Convicted, I prayed, *Lord, if that woman is waiting outside the church this week, I will know it is Your will to give her money. And I will have cash available to give her.*

Sure enough, for the third week in a row, she was there. But this time, she was standing on the far side of the parking lot. I jumped into my car and sped toward her. As I pulled into the space near her, another church member pulled up and got out to help her. *No! She's mine,* I thought. I hopped out of my car and practically pushed him out of the way. I interrupted him while he was talking with her, explaining that God had told me I was to help her.

Shocked, he stepped away.

I gave her the money I brought and asked how I could pray for her. I laid my hands on her and prayed. Mission accomplished.

But at what cost? Yes, I had followed the direction of God to give her money. But I had done God's will at the expense of hurting someone else.

As I drove away, I realized my intervention was rude, thoughtless, and prideful. It hadn't occurred to me that perhaps God wanted both of us to minister to this woman and pray for her. What made me think I was the only one who could or should help her? Instead of sharing this blessing of service, I robbed my brother of his portion.

I was ashamed of my behavior. I had done the right thing but in the wrong way. When I got home, I called my brother in Christ and apologized. I asked him to forgive me for my rudeness. As we talked, we laughed at our joint desire to help and my hyper-focus on following the will of God. I imagined my heavenly Father smiling and shaking

His head at me as I sought to do His will, but in a less-than-gracious manner.

I never saw the woman again.

Personal Reflection

- In my desire to do God's will, have I ever deprived another person from serving?

- Do I need to ask forgiveness for not valuing another's act of service?

- When I see a need and have the resources to meet it, do I ask God if I am His choice to do so?

Prayer

Today, Lord, I thank You for Your patience, mercy, and grace. Fill me with Your spirit of love. Give me a gracious heart to serve and give. Reveal to me when I close my eyes to a need instead of opening my heart and freely giving of my resources. Grant me discernment to do good deeds at the right time and in the right way. Amen.

Do not forget to show hospitality to strangers, for by so doing some people have shown hospitality to angels without knowing it. (Hebrews 13:2 NIV)

Whoever is kind to the poor lends to the LORD, and he will reward them for what they have done. (Proverbs 19:17 NIV)

What Are You Hoarding?

Brothers and sisters, I do not consider myself yet
to have taken hold of it. But one thing I do:
forgetting what is behind
and straining toward what is ahead,
I press on toward the goal to win the prize
for which God has called me heavenward
in Christ Jesus.
(Philippians 3:13–14 NIV)

What Are You Hoarding?

Honestly, I had never seen anything like it. I had heard about hoarders but had never really observed one up close. The house was barely visible due to piles of boxes, broken dishes, lamps, tables, potted plants, and various odds and ends. There was unrecognizable stuff everywhere. Each time I drove by, I thought, *If anyone lights a match, that house will go up in flames.*

When I saw the "Yard Sale" sign, I couldn't resist stopping to wander through it all. I spoke with the man who owned the house. He told me when he realized he had become a hoarder, he decided to sell all that he had accumulated. He faced the fact, made a plan, and dared to get rid of everything.

After I picked up a few items, I texted the address to my best friend, Jody. "You should drop by. You never know; you might find a surprise." Then I headed home with my treasures.

When she arrived at the place, Jody texted me, "Do you think it's safe?"

"Yes. Just browse the aisles of stuff in the front and back of the house."

"There's a house???" she responded.

I chuckled. But I felt sad too. *How does this happen?* I wondered. Surely, I would never get that bad. Admittedly, I have too many dishes, candlesticks, and vases, but they all serve a purpose. At least in my mind they do.

Matthew 7:3 (RSV), rang in my heart. "Why do you see the speck that is in your brother's eye, but do not notice the log that is in your own eye?"

I'm not a hoarder, I protested.

The Lord then confronted me with my own type of hoarding—not of material possessions, although I have too many, but emotional ones.

How many feelings of unforgiveness, anger, and resentment have I stocked up over the years? I bring them out to review whenever

I want to rationalize my less-than-righteous thoughts, sensing that I deserve better.

The Lord knows my hoarding of hurts and disappointments is far more dangerous from an eternal perspective than a physical collection of material possessions. My heart is where my Father dwells, and from it, His love should flow freely. How can anyone see my spiritual home and experience God's love through me when all the emotional clutter is blocking the way? My spiritual hoarding of grievances, lack of grace, mercy, and unforgiveness is far worse than that man's pile of stuff.

I pray I will have the courage to get rid of it all. Louise Smith, one of the first female NASCAR drivers, said, "You can't reach for anything new if your hands are still full of yesterday's junk."[5]

---

[5] Peter Economy, *17 Remarkably Inspiring Quotes to Spark Real Joy in Your Life,* (Inc. Newsletter), 4-18-2019

- Is there an old hurt or wound I keep looking at and picking over?

- Am I willing to relinquish what I have hoarded and replace it with God's presence?

- What new growth will I experience when I clear out the old for the new?

Prayer

Today, Lord, forgive me for hoarding old wounds and disappointments. Open my eyes and heart to the junk buried in my soul, and give me the courage to let it go. I want to move on and deepen my relationship with You and others. May I live each new day in the joy, freedom, and peace You have given me. Amen.

Scripture for Meditation

Let all bitterness and wrath and anger and clamor and slander be put away from you, along with all malice. Be kind to one another, tenderhearted, forgiving one another, as God in Christ forgave you. (Ephesians 4:31–32 ESV)

Forget the former things; do not dwell on the past. See, I am doing a new thing! Now it springs up; do you not perceive it? I am making a way in the wilderness and streams in the wasteland. (Isaiah 43:18–19 NIV)

Nothing is Lost
in the Sight of God

"For my thoughts are not your thoughts,

neither are your ways my ways," declares the Lord.

"As the heavens are higher than the earth,

so are my ways higher than your ways

and my thoughts than your thoughts."

(Isaiah 55:8–9 NIV)

Nothing is Lost in the Sight of God

In my childhood, whenever I couldn't find my homework or glasses, my grandmother loved saying, "Nothing is lost in the sight of God." As an adult, I remind myself of this truth each time I misplace my keys. And once, when my luggage was lost and did not arrive in Paris when I did.

Recently, I've been looking at my grandmother's favorite phrase in a new way. If material items are lost, they can be replaced. God cares much more about not losing me. He highly values my character, my relationship with Him, and my worship of Him. I may lose sight of God from time to time, but He will never lose sight of me.

Jesus told His disciples (see Matthew 10:29-31) that their heavenly Father knew even when a sparrow fell, and they were far more valuable than a little bird. Psalm 139:17–18 reminds us that God's thoughts for us are vast. He knows the longings and concerns of our hearts even before we do.

Though I seek the Lord each morning through prayer and Scripture reading to direct my day, I must confess that my checklist often takes over. I become concerned about how I will solve the challenges at hand. *I've got this.* Or so I think. But when I focus on the problem, I miss God's unique provision and purpose. When I become too busy to recognize the needs of others, and even my own, I forget to make room for Him to work, guide, and provide.

Sometimes I treat prayer casually, like a magic wand to bring my will to pass. This attitude must grieve my Lord. Godly prayer is an act of worship, surrender, and acknowledgment of who our Father is. It reveals our true intents. It also guards our hearts and minds, especially when accompanied by thanksgiving. It reminds us to look outside of ourselves to Jesus, the author and perfector of our faith (Hebrews 12:2). Prayer acknowledges that there may be a way other than the one we came up with. Submitted prayer puts Jesus in control.

When I face a problem, I want my first response to be the recognition that the solution has already been provided by my Father in heaven. This doesn't come naturally. I must give up control.

I used to pray for my desired answer to take place since I was sure it was the only logical way to solve the issue. More and more, I am asking to receive the provision or solution the Lord has waiting for me.

I want ears to hear and eyes to see the divine resolution rather than my human one. I long to practice being still and knowing He is God. (Psalm 46:10 NIV). My prayers are beginning to change from "Bless my children and my loved ones" to "Open their hearts and minds to receive the blessings that You, God, have already provided."

This prayer adjustment is small but powerful. I am changing my focus to the source. Powerful prayer is like flipping on a light switch. The electrical current is always available, but we must turn it on to receive the supply.

God created us in His image. Everything changes when we stop focusing on our human power source and trust in God's power. We make room in our lives to receive the fulfillment of the apostle Paul's prayer: "Now to Him who is able to do far more abundantly beyond all that we ask or think, according to the power that works within us" (Ephesians 3:20 NASB 95). God knows you. He sees you.

He loves you. Take delight in this assurance!

Personal Reflection

- Will I accept answers from God even when those answers are not what I prayed for?

- Do my prayers reflect a thankful heart?

- Am I letting Him be my provision?

Prayer

Today, Lord, I confess I often waste time and energy searching for more things to fill my life. Help me to rest in the truth that You provide all I need. Forgive me for filling my life with meaningless possessions and activities. Please help me to refrain from seeing a problem to be solved as more important than a person to be loved. Amen.

Scripture for Meditation

Are not two sparrows sold for a penny? Yet not one of them will fall to the ground outside your Father's care. And even the very hairs of your head are all numbered. So don't be afraid; you are worth more than many sparrows. (Matthew 10:29–31 NIV)

Do not be afraid, little flock, for your Father has chosen gladly to give you the kingdom. (Luke 12:32 NASB 95)

"For my thoughts are not your thoughts, neither are your ways my ways," declares the Lord. "As the heavens are higher than the earth, so are my ways higher than your ways and my thoughts than your thoughts." (Isaiah 55:8–9 NIV)

God's Double Delight

For me it is good to be near God;

I have made the Lord God my refuge,

that I may tell of all your works.

(Psalm 73:28 ESV)

God's Double Delight

My favorite type of rose is Double Delight. The aroma is like no other. The fragrance is sweet, fruity and has a touch of spice. The colors are a mix of vibrant fuchsia and creamy yellow. The rose has the double delight of scent and color. It is the only rose I plant in my garden. I can't have too many.

Sometimes God gives us "double delights" when He reminds us of His presence and later uses the same reminder to refresh and bless another.

Several years ago, I was having one of those mornings: tired, stressed, in a bad mood, and angry about nothing and everything. My attitude got worse throughout the day.

By mid-afternoon, I decided I needed to leave my office and get some fresh air. I walked—well, stormed, out of my office and said out loud, "God, why am I so angry?"

Just then, an enormous yellow butterfly landed on the nearby purple garlic plant. It felt like a butterfly kiss from my heavenly Father. I smiled at this delightful gift of God, which reminded me of His presence in my life. Then I laughed at myself for getting into such a negative state of mind. I went back to work feeling calm and at peace.

The following week, I attended a writers' conference where I met with a young woman who was taking appointments with attendees to help them with their social media presence. I told her about my blog, Personal Parables, where I write about spiritual applications from daily life events. She asked for an example. I started to share a recent post, but for some unknown reason, switched to the story of the butterfly, which I hadn't told anyone.

When I said the word *butterfly,* she stopped me. "What color was it?"

"It was yellow." Her eyes filled with tears when I said I felt it was God's gift to me as a reminder of His presence.

Startled by her reaction, I asked her what was wrong.

In halting words, she said her husband was ill, and she'd almost canceled her commitment to be at the conference. She asked God for a specific sign: a yellow butterfly.

I started crying right along with her. Instead of discussing social media, which now seemed completely unimportant, we prayed. I thought the butterfly was just for me, but God had a double purpose. The gift was also for my new friend, who needed reassurance of God's presence as she went through a deep trial.

God's special reminders aren't just for us. He wants us to multiply the blessing by sharing them with others. We don't always know where our stories of God's gifts will land. But every once in a while, He gives us firsthand experience. In those times, we experience the double delight of His presence in our lives and the lives of others.

Personal Reflection

- Am I consciously looking for God's gifts in my everyday life?

- What double delight has God given me lately?

- How can I be a sweet aroma of Jesus to another person?

Prayer

Today, Lord, thank You for being my loving Father and all Your gifts to me. Open my eyes and heart so I don't miss the daily delights of your presence. Help me to be a pleasing aroma of You to others. Amen.

Scripture for Meditation

The Lord is near to the brokenhearted and saves those who are crushed in spirit. (Psalm 34:18)

You will show me the path of life; in Your presence is fullness of joy; at Your right hand are pleasures forevermore. (Psalm 16:11 NKJV)

Cultivating Joy

Do not sorrow,
for the joy of the Lord is your strength.
(Nehemiah 8:10 NKJV)

Cultivating Joy

Scripture often describes our spiritual lives as a garden or a vineyard. The beautiful images of the fruit of the spirit, the vine and the branches, remind me of the need for personal cultivation, watering, pruning, and clearing away the debris so I can flourish and produce good fruit.

As I enter a time of life when there are more years behind me than before me, I often reflect on the past. There have been times when I neglected my spiritual garden. It dries up quickly and stops producing when I leave it unattended. I need to tend to it daily.

I can sow kindness and faithfulness by keeping my heart soft and my spirit strong. I can pursue peace and the living water of Jesus by studying Scripture and applying it to my life. I can pull out the spiritual weeds of worry, stress, and past hurts. When I daily pull out my spiritual weeds, chop them up, and turn them into compost, they can no longer rob me of joy.

My sister-in-law, Edwina, lived to be ninety-nine. Her life was full of the fruit of the spirit, especially love and joy. Everyone enjoyed being around her. She is my example of a woman whose strength came from her joy in the Lord. Intentional acts of "spiritual weeding" kept the garden of Edwina's life beautiful. Praise and thanksgiving through the trials of life deepened her roots and sweetened the fruit.

Even when her body was frail, she continued to produce the fruit of joy. And her joy wasn't dependent on her circumstances; it came from the Lord.

Everyone needs an Edwina to remind them, that regardless of age or physical strength, God continuously produces good fruit if we allow Him to do so. He wants to expand our gardens even when our physical world becomes smaller.

When our bodies no longer cooperate, we can use two of the most valuable tools in our spiritual garden: prayer and praise. God made us not for what we can do on our own but for what He can do in and through us. We can finish strong!

Personal Reflection

- What fruit am I cultivating in my life?

- Are there some weeds that need to be pulled out by the roots?

- What tools am I using to enhance the growth of my spiritual life?

Prayer

Today, Lord, I thank You for being the perfect gardener. You prune me to clear away the weeds that entangle my thoughts. You help me thrive, shine, and reflect Your image. Show me daily the areas of my life that need pruning. Help me cultivate my soul's soil to mirror Your love and joy. Amen

Scripture for Meditation

You will go out in joy and be led forth in peace; the mountains and hills will burst into song before you, and all the trees of the field will clap their hands. (Isaiah 55:12 NIV)

May the God of hope fill you with all joy and peace as you trust in

him, so that you may overflow with hope by the power of the Holy

Spirit. (Romans 15:13 NIV)

What Blessings Am I Missing?

How many are your works, Lord!
In wisdom you made them all;
the earth is full of your creatures.
There is the sea, vast and spacious,
teeming with creatures beyond number—
living things both large and small.
(Psalm 104:24-25 NIV)

What Blessings Am I Missing?

There are times of the year that represent joyful expectations for me. I love the sights, the sounds, and the celebrations with friends and family as one year ends and another begins. However, it is easy for me to get caught up in the preparations, especially at Christmas, and overlook the real Gift—Emmanuel, God with us. I can become so busy doing that that I forget to be and rest in the presence of Christ Himself. Every year, I vow it will be different. Yet, I drift into old habits of busyness.

In my quiet time one year, I asked God, Am I too busy? Too stretched and trying to do too much? The answer was a resounding YES. I know this because I woke up the next day sick. Now I had to stop, and it was a good thing. I did need to rest, sort out my thoughts, and evaluate what was important. I want to be still and listen to God but I struggle with it most of the time.

My heart desires to experience the gift of Jesus every day and not just at Christmas. I want to experience the daily gift of His presence. I want to have eyes to see His blessings each day in the ordinary and expected, as well as the unexpected and extraordinary.

One summer, when my husband and I decided to take a back road on a busy holiday to avoid traffic, we experienced a surprise. There was no one on the road, just cattle grazing, wandering deer, and soaring birds. We were relaxed and peaceful.

As we came around a corner, suddenly there was a massive herd of sheep; a surprising change from the cattle. More surprising was the rancher, sitting in his farm equipment, playing the saxophone while overlooking the sheep! A delightful God gift out in the middle of nowhere. We would have missed it if we had taken the main road.

Sometimes we are privileged to receive a gift from God as we witness a holy moment. One evening, while serving at our local homeless shelter. A young man came through the line and asked for two plates of food. One for an elderly man who was having trouble walking and one for himself. He said if he could only have one plate, he would give it to the old man and return to the end of the line for himself. Of course, I gave him two plates.

This kindness was sweet enough, but then I watched as this young man sat with the old man. The two of them were alone at a table. The young man was leaning in, listening, and very engaged with the old man. Later in the evening, he asked for something softer for the man to eat because the man was having trouble chewing.

The tenderness of this young man was for me a holy moment. It was as if I were watching Jesus tenderly care for one of his children. This homeless young man had such compassion as he ministered to the older homeless man. I realized I was watching something extraordinary, very holy. It was Jesus in action. This young man was giving the equivalent of a cup of cold water to the least of them. It might have seemed that those of us serving were the givers. But the truth was, the one who gave the most that night was the young man who gave what he had: time, love, mercy, and compassion.

The scripture is full of ordinary people who God used to do the extraordinary. David was a shepherd, Mary was a young Jewish girl, and Peter was a fisherman. God chose them to be extraordinary for the Lord.

Can you imagine what it was like for Mary? She may have been just a young girl to those around her, but God had other plans. Everything changed when the angels announced she would bear a son, the Son! From that moment, her ordinary life became extraordinary. In the song "Mary did you know?" there is a verse that asks, "Did you know that your baby boy has come to make you new? This child that you've delivered, will soon deliver you?" When I take the time to think about this, to be still and truly reflect, it takes my breath away. Jesus, our Savior, chose to reveal Himself as a baby to a young girl. He chose then, as He often does now, to reveal Himself in the ordinary.

The angel told Mary her Son was special, but for most of her life, she didn't see the fullness of the promise until His resurrection. So it is with us. We often don't see or understand what God is doing in our lives until many years later, as we reflect and see His hand and His purpose. In the meantime, we trust in the promise of things unseen.

Personal Reflection

- What areas of my life are consumed with preparations and missing the blessing of God's presence?

- What is one change I can make today to remove unnecessary busyness?

- Am I looking for opportunities to be a blessing as I encounter Jesus in ordinary moments?

Prayer

Today, Lord, open my heart to your presence in ordinary moments. Forgive me for looking for "big moments" instead of encountering you in the simple moments. Thank you for being present in my life each day. Please help me be a blessing to others. Amen.

Scripture for Meditation

The Lord is near to all who call upon Him, to all who call upon Him in truth. (Psalm 145:18)

When I look at your heavens, the work of your fingers, the moon and

the stars, which you have set in place, what is man that you are mindful

of him, and the son of man that you care for him? (Psalm 8:3-4 ESV)

What Are You Choosing?

By grace you have been saved through faith,
and that not of yourselves; it is the gift of God,
not of works, lest anyone should boast.
(Ephesians 2:8–9 NKJV)

What Are You Choosing?

Are certain celebrations or holidays in your life full of contradictions? They are for me. I love Christmas and Easter. But they often involve a mix of great joy and profound sadness, usually due to unmet expectations. My heart is sorrowful when all my children and grandchildren aren't with me to celebrate the birth and resurrection of my Lord. In these conflicting emotions, I must choose between focusing on the desires of my heart and the purpose of the celebration: Jesus.

Some years are easier than others. But the process is the same: reflect on God's love and His decision to send Jesus, His only begotten Son, to die for my sins. My perspective changes when I meditate on the miracle of God becoming flesh to live among us.

Jesus's willingness to become one of us began a continuum of action that ultimately led to the choice, commitment, and completion at the cross. At any point, Jesus could have said, "This is too much, too hard, too painful." But He didn't.

Even in His choice to be obedient, He was honest and vulnerable. He went to the Father and said, "If You are willing, remove this cup from Me," then added, "Yet not My will, but Yours be done" (Luke 22:42). By praying this prayer, Jesus modeled transparency and honesty for us. He went to His Father with a sincere desire to avoid the cruelty of the cross.

Jesus understood the cross was the only way for us to receive forgiveness for our sins. He accepted the arduous and painful path. Scripture says, "For the joy set before Him, He endured the cross, despising the shame" (Hebrews 12:2 NASB 95).

Jesus showed us how to look beyond the raw emotional and physical pain to gain the prize. For Jesus, it was sitting "at the right hand of the throne of God" (Hebrews 12:2). For us, it is "the prize of the upward call of God in Christ Jesus" (Philippians 3:14). God's eternal purpose is for us to be holy and blameless, and we can only obtain that by faith in Christ. Even faith is not our own; it is the gift of God (Ephesians 2:8). It is a gift of grace.

We can choose to accept this gift or not, to follow the will of God or not. Sometimes the decision feels too hard, too painful. Like Jesus, we can go to our Father and pour out our fears, our trepidations, and our desire for an easier road. But when we come to the same acceptance—"Not my will, but Yours be done"—we find He has carved a path for us and shines His light to show us the way.

He has provided everything He asks of us.

- He tells us to love as He loved. We can only do this because He loved us first (1 John 4:19)

- He tells us to be faithful, but He is the author and finisher of our faith (Hebrews 12:2)

- He tells us it is better to serve than to be served. He models service when He washed the disciples' feet, even the feet of the one who would betray Him. (John 13:1–30)

God provides the very things that He requires of us. When troubles come, He reminds us that His yoke is easy and His burden is light (Matthew 11:30). Greater is He who is in us than he who is in the world (1 John 4:4). He chose us, and we choose Him. It is a circle of choosing.

Whatever you've experienced in prior years, Jesus was with you in the joys and the sorrows. Thank Him for His blessings and offer a sacrifice of praise for the disappointments. Choose to live in the light of Christ and His truth rather than the darkness of the world.

Personal Reflection

- Will I choose to follow the light of Jesus today?

- What specific choices will I make to keep Jesus the center of my life?

- Who can I encourage to join me in following Jesus in a new and fresh way?

Prayer

Today, Lord, I remember that You made this day and this year. I choose to be glad and rejoice in them and in You, my light, my provision, and my salvation. Amen.

Scripture for Meditation

Then they came to a place which was named Gethsemane; and He said to His disciples, "Sit here while I pray." And He took Peter, James, and John with Him, and He began to be troubled and deeply distressed. Then He said to them, "My soul is exceedingly sorrowful, even to death. Stay here and watch." He went a little farther, and fell on the ground, and prayed that if it were possible, the hour might pass from Him. And He said, "Abba, Father, all things are possible for You. Take this cup away from Me; nevertheless, not what I will, but what You will." (Mark 14:32–36 NKJV)

We love because He first loved us. (1 John 4:19)

What Delights You?

The Lord takes delight in his people;

he crowns the humble with victory.

(Psalm 149:4 NIV)

What Delights You?

I love saying the word delightful. The word feels joyful to me. *Delight,* according to *Merriam-Webster's Online Dictionary,* means "to take great pleasure" or "to give keen enjoyment" in something or someone.[6]

One of my delights is the unabashed joy of children playing. They run, giggle, and never worry about their appearance or how they sound. Without hesitation, they savor the moment.

Jesus said, "Therefore, whoever will humble himself like this child, is the greatest in the kingdom of heaven" (Matthew 18:4). He asks us adults to come to Him with the innocence and trust of a child. He is not asking us to be childish but childlike. Come without reservation, without thought, with abandonment, into His presence. Soak up His love as children soak up the rain when it pours over them.

---

[6] "Delight," *Merriam-Webster.com Dictionary*, Merriam-Webster, https://www.merriam-webster.com/dictionary/delight. Accessed February 25, 2025

Not only does our heavenly Father want us to delight in Him, but He delights in us! Isn't that incredible? The Creator of the universe takes great pleasure in His children. He enjoys us. What amazing love!

Lift your heart and soak in the blessings of being a child of the King who can reach up toward heaven and say, "Abba, Father, thank You for loving me just as I am."

Personal Reflection

- How will I find delight today in the love of Jesus?

- How can I encourage others to delight in being children of God?

- Is there an area of my life I need to let go of to experience childlike faith in Jesus?

Prayer

Today, Lord, I thank You for loving me tenderly and unconditionally. Help me to delight in Your presence with abandonment and faith, knowing You are entirely trustworthy. Amen.

Scripture for Meditation

Jesus said, "Let the little children come to me, and do not hinder them, for the kingdom of heaven belongs to such as these." (Matthew 19:14 NIV)

Delight yourself also in the Lord, and He shall give you the desires of your heart. (Psalm 37:4 NKJV)

Listen to the Music

We love, because He first loved us.

(1 John 4:19)

Years ago, I received a creative and unique Valentine's gift: ten cassette tapes (remember those?) filled with music and marked A through R. The only instruction was to listen to all the tapes in alphabetical order. Oh, my goodness, that's a lot of time and music. And it was tax season, the busiest time of year for me. But I followed the instructions. It took me about six weeks to listen to the entire set.

The first song was "Listen to the Music." As I listened, I realized there was a theme to the collection. Each song was a bit more personal than the one before. The final two songs were "I Will Always Love You" and "Can I Have This Dance for the Rest of My Life?" My sweet, shy boyfriend was proposing. I accepted, and we spent thirty-one wonderful years together.

God proposes to us throughout Scripture. From Genesis to Revelation, He speaks of His eternal love for us. He declares His plans for our good. And ultimately, He gives His only Son, Jesus, who surrendered His life so that you and I could spend eternity with Him. The lover of our souls says, "Listen to My music, My voice, as I tell of My love for you. I want you to spend the rest of your life, including eternity, with Me, the Creator of the universe."

What an amazing invitation! Will you listen to God and accept His proposal?

May your life and heart be filled with the love of Jesus.

Personal Reflection

- How am I listening for God's voice?

- Do I invest time each day to nurture my relationship with my Creator?

- What is one act I can do today to draw closer to Jesus?

Prayer

Today, Lord, thank You for Your everlasting love. Help me to never lose sight of Your mercy, grace, and comfort. May my life and lips proclaim Your goodness in all I do and say. Amen.

Scripture for Meditation

The Lord your God in your midst, the Mighty One, will save; He will rejoice over you with gladness, He will quiet you with His love, He will rejoice over you with singing. (Zephaniah 3:17 NKJV)

But God, who is rich in mercy, because of His great love with which He loved us, even when we were dead in trespasses, made us alive together with Christ (by grace you have been saved). (Ephesians 2:4–5 NKJV)

Acknowledgements

Writing a book is a labor of love. But it requires the help, prayers and support of many.

To my Lord and Savior, Jesus, thank you for your daily presence, especially in the ordinary moments. Thank you for bringing scripture to life and opening up opportunities to share your love and salvation with others.

My precious husband, Rick, who always supported me in every area of my life. He was my mentor, my dearest friend, my love. I miss you.

Catherine O'Brien continues to be my unseen but irreplaceable partner in all my writing and speaking endeavors. She prays with and for me, encourages me, listens when I am unsure and bravely lets me know when I am off track. She "gets me." I am grateful beyond words.

My family who continues to love and support me in season and out. They are a gift and example to me of unconditional love.

Thank you to my edit readers and friends, Jody Landon, Ann Little, Deena Pangborn, Kathleen Schmidt, Sue Huntley and Mandy Piper. Thank you for your keen eye and suggestions. A special thanks to Kathy Ide, who edited the first of several drafts of this book. Any errors or mistakes are all mine, not Kathy's. She encouraged and taught me during this process.

My Personal Parables readers who encouraged me to compile my blogs into a book. Your monthly feedback means the world to me as I seek to write words that will encourage you to seek Jesus in every aspect of your life; in the ordinary and extraordinary moments.

Thank you to my son and daughter in law, Ryan and Tracy Rogers for the inspiration of this beautiful book cover, along with Crystal Mayo who finalized my vision. This was a collaboration of ideas, inspiration and love.

Special thanks to Bob and Catherine O'Brien for the title concept and to Jody Landon, Jan Marrett and Jeannie Malik, special friends who are always ready to listen when I just need to talk things out again and then again. I am blessed.

Final Thoughts to My Readers

I hope you have been inspired and encouraged to encounter Jesus every day and in every ordinary moment.

If you have read this book but have not made a personal commitment to Jesus, this is the time. He gave His life for you and for me. Please accept His love, His forgiveness, His provision by asking Him into your life. Don't wait. Do it now.